# ADELPHI PAPERS
NUMBER ONE HUNDRED AND SEVENTY-NINE

# Greek Security: Issues and Politics

*by Thanos Veremis*

THE INTERNATIONAL INSTITUTE FOR STRATEGIC STUDIES
23 TAVISTOCK STREET LONDON WC2E 7NQ

ADELPHI PAPER No. 179

This Paper was written when the author was a Research Associate at the IISS. He is currently a Lecturer in Modern Greek History at the Panteios School of Political Science.

The views expressed in this Paper are the author's own and should not be taken to represent the views of the Institute or its members.

First published Winter 1982

ISBN 0 86079 065 7
ISSN 0567-932X

© The International Institute for Strategic Studies 1982

All rights reserved. No part of this publication may be reproduced, stored in a retrieval system, or transmitted in any form or by any means, electronic, mechanical, photo-copying, recording or otherwise, without the prior permission of the International Institute for Strategic Studies.

*The International Institute for Strategic studies was founded in 1958 as a centre for the provision of information on and research into the problems of international security, defence and arms control in the nuclear age. It is international in its Council and staff, and its membership is drawn from over fifty countries. It is independent of governments and is not the advocate of any particular interest.*

*The Institute is concerned with strategic questions – not just with the military aspects of security but with the social and economic sources and political moral implications of the use and existence of armed force: in other words with the basic problems of peace.*

*The Institute's publications are intended for a much wider audience than its own membership and are available to the general public on subscription or singly.*

Printed in Great Britain by Adlard & Son Ltd, Bartholomew Press, Dorking

# CONTENTS

| | |
|---|---|
| INTRODUCTION | 1 |
| I. THE CONDITIONS OF GREEK SECURITY | 3 |
|     The Region | 3 |
|     The Soviet Threat and NATO | 4 |
|     Turkey | 5 |
| II. GREEK SECURITY PROBLEMS AND POLICIES | 6 |
|     Relations with the Balkan States | 6 |
|     Graeco–Turkish Relations | 9 |
|     Greek Relations with the US and NATO | 16 |
| III. DOMESTIC FACTORS | 23 |
|     PASOK | 23 |
|     The New Democracy Party | 25 |
|     The Centre Union Party | 26 |
|     The Communist Party | 26 |
|     The Role of the Armed Forces | 27 |
|     Economic Aspects of Greek Security | 30 |
| IV. THE NATURE OF GREEK SECURITY IN THE 1980s | 32 |
|     The Link with the West and Turkey | 32 |
|     The Soviet and Communist Threat | 35 |
|     Future Prospects and Security Options for Greece | 36 |
| NOTES | 39 |

# Greek Security: Issues and Politics

## INTRODUCTION

The security priorities of small states in strategic locations not only concern great powers but are often defined by them. The latter's influence may be exerted either directly or through organizations of collective security, and it is not an uncommon feature of such organizations to equate the interests of its junior members with those of its senior. The equation may rest unchallenged as long as the benefits of the relationship continue to exceed the liabilities. However, when a crisis of incompatibility arises between great-power prescriptions and the perceived interests of the smaller states, the future of the relationship will depend largely on the flexibility of the great-power. It is precisely Greece's attempt to redefine her security priorities and the response of the Western Alliance to such an attempt which are the main themes of this Paper.

Since 1974, Greece has capitalized on the loosening of the international system in order to conduct a more independent foreign policy intended to cope with the perceived threats to Greek security from Turkey and the Warsaw Pact. Problems arise because American and NATO officials would deny the threat to Greece's interests from Turkey and make more of the Warsaw Pact threat, and would seem unwilling to comprehend that Greek threat perceptions are not simply the whim of domestic politics.

The Elections of 18 October 1981 gave the 'Panhellenic Socialist Movement' (PASOK) under Andreas Papandreou a clear mandate. To what extent Papandreou will carry out his promise to revise Greek ties with the European Community and withdraw from NATO remains to be seen, but he has already made it clear that his Administration will not follow in the footsteps of its predecessor.

The United States and NATO rely considerably on bases in Greece for the support of the Sixth Fleet and the US Air Forces. Greece also provides intelligence and communications links between Turkey and Western Europe, nuclear weapons storage, and facilities for exercises and training. The storage of fuel and ammunition for the replenishment of American naval and air forces is important for the functioning of these forces in peace and war. Greece's own security considerations should therefore merit greater Western attention than they have received. However, before analysing recent developments in Greek security politics, a brief historical perspective is necessary to demonstrate the continuity of these policies.

**Historical Background**

Limited national sovereignty and dependence on guarantor powers were common features of the Balkan states that emerged into statehood in the nineteenth century. Their foreign policies evolved in conjunction with the dynamics of European politics and the security arrangements of the major powers – Britain, France, Russia, Austria and, after 1866, Germany and Italy. Conflicting Balkan claims on the European possessions of the declining Ottoman Empire were also drawn into the realm of international antagonisms.

The two most persistent, but mutually exclusive, Greek security problems have concerned the Turks and the Balkan Slavs. After the establishment of her independence in 1830, Greece did not give up her claims on Ottoman territories with sizeable Greek populations. The welfare and security of these people became a primary concern of the new state, and their discontent was a constant cause of friction between Greece and the Ottoman Empire. After 1869 the Ottomans embarked on a policy of exploiting the inherent rivalries among the Balkan claimants for their European possessions. By the end of the nineteenth century, the religious struggle between adherents of the autonomous Bulgarian Exarchate Church and the followers of the Greek Patriarch in Macedonia developed into a covert conflict between Greece and Bulgaria.[1] The major predicament of Greek foreign policy at the beginning of the twentieth century became to adjudicate priorities between her two major, and often conflicting, security concerns – the liberation of Greek populations from Ottoman rule on the one hand, and preventing the Bulgarians from dominating Macedonia on the other.

The Balkan Wars of 1912–13 and World War I (which did not end for Greece until 1922) resolved most of the outstanding differences between the Balkan participants. The Treaty of Lausanne, signed in 1923, ended the era of Greek irredentism and signified the beginning of Greece's internal development. One and a half million refugees from Asia Minor descended upon a country of less than five million as a consequence of Greek defeat by the Nationalist Turkish forces, and this had a direct impact on the country. The urban refugees provided cheap labour for the growing industrial sector and brought skills useful for the development of the economy. The rural refugees settled mostly in Macedonia and Thrace and promoted the linguistic and ethnic homogeneity of these regions after the voluntary exodus of Bulgarians and the compulsory exchange of the Macedonian Turks.

The power vacuum in the Balkans and the Eastern Mediterranean created by World War I gave Italy the opportunity to pursue her interests in that region without opposition, but the improvement of relations with Italy in 1928 gave Greece some respite to deal with her other Balkan concerns. In 1930 an Accord was signed by Kemal Atatürk and Prime Minister Venizelos which settled outstanding matters between Greece and Turkey and began a tacit relationship which lasted longer than any other in the inter-war period in the Balkans.

In February 1934 a Treaty was signed between Greece, Romania, Yugoslavia and Turkey. This was heralded as a triumph of Balkan co-operation, though, because it was shunned by Albania and Bulgaria, the Treaty did not secure the signatories from external threats but virtually invited the European powers to involve themselves in Balkan disputes. Venizelos, whose policy had been to ensure Greece's integrity in case of any international conflagration, was critical of the multilateralism of his successor, P. Tsaldaris. Venizelos' main concern while in office had been to avoid a war with Italy if the latter attacked Yugoslavia through Albania. His fears were not unfounded. The rift between Britain and Italy after the Abyssinian Crisis of 1935 and Greece's willingness to attach herself inextricably to British interests (in spite of Britain's reluctance to provide guarantees of alliance) had paved the way for the Italian attack of October 1940. Ioannis Metaxas, appointed Dictator by King George II in 1936, displayed a constancy towards Britain which was only rivalled by that of his anglophile royal patron.[2]

In the Winter of 1940 the Greek army repelled an Italian surprise attack and, after a successful counter-offensive, pinned down the Italian forces deep inside Albanian territory. Between 5 April and the end of that month, German armoured divisions, coming to the help of the Italians, overran Yugoslavia and Greece. The King and his Ministers, along with what could be salvaged of the armed forces, were evacuated to Crete, and after that island also fell a government-in-exile was established in London and Cairo.

Greece's resistance to invasion, and the subsequent British presence in that country forced Hitler's Germany to embark on a Balkan campaign, thereby disrupting the timetable of her attack on the Soviet Union.[3] The Greeks were proud of their contribution to the Allied cause, but the terrible price they were subsequently forced to pay fuelled their resentment of a royalist regime which had long denied them their political rights. For many, resistance was a war against both occupying forces and authoritarianism in general. The reluctance of the exiled Government to recognize the extent of anti-monarchist sentiment in Greece increased the influence of the Communist-led broad-based resistance movement EAM–ELAS and precipitated a devastating conflict between royalist and anti-royalist officers in the Greek Army in the Middle East and North Africa.

An aggressive EAM–ELAS policy of monopolizing the resistance, and the incompatibility of Communist political goals with British commitment to the constitutional monarchy, brought about an internal confrontation after the German withdrawal during which some of the smaller Republican resistance groups sided with the repatriated Government and the British against the Communists.

In 1946 the first elections for ten years were held in circumstances hardly conducive to parliamentary politics. The KKE (Greek Communist Party) abstained, thus ensuring victory for the right-wing parties – which promptly conducted the plebiscite which brought back King George. The disorientated liberals, increasingly isolated in the middle of a polarized political scene, threw in their lot with the royalists in the civil war which broke out between right-of-centre nationalists and Communists. This armed conflict, which continued from 1946 to 1949, inflicted the worst punishment on the country since the War of Independence. Its legacy in material loss was no less appalling than its long-term effect on Greek society and politics.

In 1947, Stalin, who had until then honoured his 1944 agreement with Churchill to allow Britain a free hand in Greece, demanded the withdrawal of British troops. He also sought revision of the 1936 Montreux Convention, which defines the regime of the Dardanelles, and raised claims over the Dodecanese Islands which were ceded to Greece in 1947.[4]

Between 1946 and 1948 British influence gave way to US influence in Greece. In March 1947 the Truman Doctrine declared US intentions to prevent Greece and Turkey from passing under Soviet control. For the US, Greece became the first testing ground – and indeed the first battle-ground – of the Cold War Doctrine. Besides military aid, the US supplied military advisers and formed a joint General Staff with the Greek Government to conduct operations. In the UN General Assembly, Albania, Yugoslavia and Bulgaria were condemned for aiding the Communist forces, but in fact it was Tito's break with the Cominform in 1948 which deprived the Greek Communist forces of their strategic exit to Yugoslavia and of Yugoslav support. By the Autumn of 1949 the Government forces held the field.

War, enemy occupation and civil strife had brought Greece disaster to a degree hardly paralleled elsewhere in Europe. Central and local administration was paralyzed; the economic infrastructure was shattered; inflation was out of control. As Campbell states, 'Dependence on great powers which had characterised Greece's history since the establishment of the modern states was never more evident than in her reliance on the American presence during these years to preserve the Greek version of parliamentary government and free economy'.[5]

## I. THE CONDITIONS OF GREEK SECURITY

**The Region**
The Mediterranean, extending from Gibraltar to the Dardanelles and the Suez Canal, covers 1.5 million square kilometres. It connects three members of the Southern Region of NATO, which is the largest area in Allied Command Europe, 4,000 km from East to West and some 1,400 km from the Alps to the coast of Libya.[1] About one tenth of the world's population resides in the states bordering the sea – on which 1,500 ocean-going ships and some 5,000 smaller craft travel on an average day. The Mediterranean is also the junction of three Continents, three major religious communities (Christian, Moslem and Jewish), two major military and ideological blocs and a number of non-aligned states. It is also an important route for west-bound Middle East oil pumped to Eastern Mediterranean pipeline terminals, as well as for oil exported to Europe from North African producers.[2]

Europe and the United States have a vital interest in maintaining the *status quo* in the Mediterranean and especially in its more troubled eastern part. The priorities of the West in the region include the protection of oil interests, the prevention of a crisis over

Israel which might endanger relations with Saudi Arabia, and the containment of Soviet influence and incursion. The Sixth Fleet and American bases in various littoral states are both political instruments and a deterrent against the Soviet Union. The Fleet normally comprises two aircraft-carrier groups and some fifteen surface combatants, varying from cruisers to escorts, and one main amphibious unit – although recently one carrier task force has been on temporary duty in the Indian Ocean. The aircraft carriers each have eighty to ninety combat aircraft, some of which have a nuclear strike role. These aircraft have a combat radius of 600 to 800 km, thus covering land targets in the southern Soviet Union. NATO tactical air units, nuclear stockpiles and communication networks also contribute to the Western military presence in the region.[3]

The major installations used by the United States in Greece include the Hellenikon air base in Athens, the Nea Makri communications station near Marathon, the Iraklion air station and the Suda Bay complex in Crete. Other US communications facilities and five NATO Air Defence in the Ground Environment (NADGE) sites are spread throughout the country, mainly in the north of Greece. There are also nuclear weapons and storage sites dating from the 1960s. The missiles are held in Greek bases with the warheads under US control.

The most important of these facilities is generally acknowledged to be the Suda Bay complex, which houses fuel and ammunition for use by US and NATO naval forces. The Bay provides port facilities, an anchorage which can accommodate most of the Sixth Fleet if necessary and an airfield for use by American military reconnaissance aircraft. The NATO missile firing range at nearby Namfi, where training and testing exercises are conducted, is associated with the Suda complex.

The Iraklion air station supports reconnaissance flights and the refuelling of US aircraft. Also associated with Iraklion is an electronic surveillance station manned by the US Air Force Security Service (USAFSS). This listening post monitors Soviet activities in the eastern Mediterranean.

The Hellenikon air base serves as a headquarters and provides support for other US Air Force Europe (USAFE) facilities in Greece. Electronic and photographic reconnaissance missions are mounted from this base, which is also the staging point for air transport operations of USAFE, and it also provides support for the US Military Airlift Command (MAC).[4]

Nea Makri houses a major communications centre which is part of the global US Defense Communications System (DCS). The centre is tied into the Licola terminal at Naples, Italy, and the Morón terminal in Spain. The Kato Souli terminal near Nea Makri is linked with the Sixth Fleet and with bases in Naples and Spain. Mount Pateras, 20 miles West of Athens, is believed to connect Greece with the Yamanlar terminal near Izmir, Turkey, and provides a link between North-east Crete, the island of Lefkas in the Ionian Sea and a terminal in southern Italy.[5]

**The Soviet Threat and NATO**

In strictly regional terms, the Soviet Union appears to be more interested in diminishing the threat posed to her own security than in competing with the United States for supremacy. Through 'carrot and cannon tactics' the Soviet Union has secured passage by way of the Dardanelles into the Mediterranean. The Soviet naval squadron based at Sebastopol on the Black Sea is deployed in the Mediterranean, spending much of its time at deep water anchorages near choke-points of the Mediterranean, and it also has use of port facilities at Tartus and Latakia (Syria) and limited repair facilities at Tirat (Yugoslavia). The rapid growth of the Fifth Escadra during the past ten years has reflected a general Soviet projection of power at sea. The Escadra comprises up to 15–20 major surface combatants, amphibious landing craft and auxiliary vessels. Its nuclear and diesel-powered submarines (up to 10) come from the Soviet Northern Fleet. To compensate for lack of regular access to ports, Soviet warships make extensive use of shoals in international waters where the sea is shallow enough to permit the anchoring of large vessels and the rendezvous with oilers and supply ships.[6] The Soviet Union has established anchorages and maintenance facilities ten to eleven miles from the low tide-mark off the coasts of Anticythira, St Eustratios and Crete. An extension of Greek territorial waters will require Graeco-Soviet consultations leading to one of two possible solutions: either the Soviet facilities will remain in operation within Greek territorial waters and thus will be regarded as foreign military installations, or these facilities will have to be removed. It is safe therefore to assume that the Soviet Union would oppose such an extension, unless she were given guarantees of uninterrupted tenure. In case of such a development it would be expected that the US and NATO would react adversely to an official 'co-existence' of their bases along with Soviet facilities in Greek territory.[7]

In spite of the expansion of Soviet naval presence in the Eastern Mediterranean between 1970 and 1980 the USSR continues to lack significant sea-based and land-based air power. This obstacle has been partly overcome by the appearance of naval *Backfire* bombers, based in the Crimea, which can cover most of the Mediterranean basin. The introduction of this aircraft has increased the importance of the number and quality of Greek and Turkish air defence fighters.

The Warsaw Pact has also expanded and modernized its land forces facing NATO's Southern Flank. Some 33 Warsaw Pact divisions are deployed on the Graeco-Turkish borders against a total of 25 Greek and Turkish divisions. The Pact possesses an advantage of three-to-one in terms of mechanized and armoured capability.[8] The Soviet Union has also deployed intermediate-range ballistic missiles (IRBM), including the SS-20 with three multiple independently targetable re-entry vehicles (MIRV), in the Crimea and in the Northern Transcaucasus.[9] As part of NATO's Theatre Nuclear Force (TNF) modernization, ground-launched cruise missiles (GLCM) are to be deployed at Comiso in Sicily in the mid-1980s.

## Turkey

Greece's post-war defence was primarily directed against both an internal and external Communist threat. Her northern borders with Albania, Yugoslavia and Bulgaria originally attracted the almost exclusive attention of military planners and, through her association with the United States and NATO, Greece's security concerns were incorporated into the larger scheme of Western collective security. However, the Graeco-Turkish dispute over Cyprus, compounded in 1974 by the Turkish invasion of the island, drastically altered Greece's security orientation. Besides the Cyprus issue, three other critical questions have given rise to serious tension between the two NATO allies: *1)* Turkey's demands over the Aegean continental shelf; *2)* the air-space dispute; and *3)* the reallocation of operational responsibilities of the Aegean sea and air space. These are discussed below.

At the centre of Greek concern over Turkish claims in the Aegean is the security of the islands formally ceded to Greece in 1923 and 1947. Turkey, while facing the Greek islands with the second largest fleet of landing craft in NATO and a newly constructed Fourth (Aegean) Army, accuses Greece of violating articles of the Lausanne and Paris Treaties by militarizing her islands off the coast of Asia Minor. Prominent Turks, such as former Defence Minister Sancar, former Prime Minister Demirel, former Minister of Foreign Affairs Esenbel and former Vice-Premier Turkes, have made undisguised references to Turkish 'rights' and claims on the Greek islands. If Turkey eventually succeeded in controlling contiguous Greek islands, her strategic value would be increased, and, with control of the entire sea approaches to the Dardanelles, her bargaining position *vis-à-vis* the two superpowers would be considerably enhanced. Greece's current security concern is to safeguard her sovereign island territories.

More than any other country in the region Greece's economy is dependent on the sea. Half her population of nine million live in three major Mediterranean ports – Athens (Piraeus), Thessaloniki and Patras – and most of their inhabitants are employed directly or indirectly in trades connected with the sea. Greek concern over the welfare of the islands should not be underestimated. Moreover, the prospect of a Turkish population of about 70 million by the end of the century adds to Greek anxieties.[10]

## II. GREEK SECURITY PROBLEMS AND POLICIES

There is a historical continuity to Greece's security problems which is underlined by her geopolitical significance. Although World War II altered the social regimes of her northern neighbours, some of the issues which have traditionally caused strife among these states themselves and between them and Greece are still active today. However, the intensity of conflict has depended on the condition of Soviet–American relations. The era of detente improved relations between Greece and her Balkan neighbours, but it was ultimately disillusionment with United States policy during the Junta period and the subsequent conflict with Turkey that was to bring about a partial emancipation of Greek foreign policy.

**Relations with the Balkan States**
The issue of the ethnic balance of Greek Macedonia was resolved with the exchanges of populations between 1920 and 1923.[1] The overwhelming preponderance of the Greek element in Macedonia, enhanced by 700,000 Greek refugees from Asia Minor, could not be disputed, yet the KKE – badly split over the issue – was forced by the Comintern during the Sixth Balkan Communist Conference in 1924 to underwrite the Bulgarian slogan for a 'united and Independent Macedonia and Thrace'.[2] This policy, which amounted to the ceding of Greek Macedonia to a state under Bulgarian influence, was abandoned in 1935 but caused irreparable damage to the image of the Communist Party at home.

After German occupation, Bulgaria in practice incorporated most of Eastern Macedonia and Western Thrace without the formality of declaring war on Greece. In Western Macedonia the German authorities gave the Bulgarians a free hand in propaganda and intimidation of the local population. Greek resistance forces were confronted with a double struggle, against the occupying army as well as against the parliamentary Bulgarian nationalist battalions (Ohrana). In 1943, at a conference between Yugoslavia and Greek partisans, Tito's representatives for the first time used the term 'Macedonian nationals' and sought EAM–ELAS co-operation in order to win Bulgarian collaborators back to the 'Macedonian' ideological camp. Although ELAS refused the Yugoslavs the right to organize Greek Slavophone resistance groups, they agreed to include them in their resistance movement and later granted them the option of forming their own units of the Slav Macedonian National Liberation Front (SNOF) under ELAS command.[3]

Yugoslav plans to form a Macedonian state under Yugoslavian dominance, to include the Bulgarian Pirin Macedonia (and the Greek 'Aegean' Macedonia), were naturally not welcomed by the Bulgarian Communist regime after World War II, but the relative weakness of the Soviet-liberated country, as opposed to the triumphant partisan regime of her neighbour, did not permit overt opposition. Until Tito's break with the Cominform in 1948, Yugoslavia enjoyed a period of unqualified preponderance, and Tito's 'Macedonian' policy was to a considerable degree accepted by the Dimitrov regime in Bulgaria.

Discussions of a South Slav Federation between Yugoslavia and Bulgaria were concluded in the Bled Protocols of 1947, the high point in the co-operation between the two states. It was implied in the Agreements that the Pirin Macedonians (as well as their Aegean 'brethren') would be granted cultural autonomy as a first step towards their incorporation in the People's Republic of Macedonia. The Bulgarians reluctantly kept their side of the Agreement, but the Greek Communists were in no position to agree to such decisions, and the Greek Government had by then severed its communications with the Communist states.[4]

Until 1948 the Bulgarian Government kept a low profile on the issue of Greek Macedonia, reiterating its claims to Western Thrace and demands for an exit into the Aegean. These claims had been supported at the Paris Peace Conference of 1946 by both the Soviet Union and Yugoslavia. However, the clash between Stalin and Tito had a profound effect on the entire nexus of Balkan politics. Yugoslavia terminated her support for the Greek Communist guerrillas who continued to keep faith (though inconspicuously) with the Cominform. Seeking a way out of isolation and encirclement by hostile Communist states, Tito signed the death warrant of the 'Greek Communist Democratic Army' and proceeded to improve relations with the Greek Government.

The KKE split badly over Yugoslavia's rebellion. Zachariades, the powerful Chairman of the Greek Communist Party, upheld Cominform orthodoxy and cashiered his Commander-in-Chief, taking over his office while pro-Yugoslav elements and certain other Slav-speaking groups fled to Yugoslavia. At the fifth plenum of its Central Committee in January 1949 the leadership of the KKE endorsed the new Cominform policy for the establishment of an independent Macedonia within a Balkan Federation. This return to the 1924 position remained the party line until it was officially abandoned in 1956. In August 1949 the 'Democratic Army' was heavily defeated and, along with Slavophone supporters, sought refuge first in Albania and then in other Communist countries.

The Bulgarian Government was quick to repudiate the content of the Bled Protocols and declared that their Pirin district was part of a Bulgarian-sponsored autonomous Macedonia. The teaching of the Macedonian dialect was banned, and all traces of Yugoslav propaganda among the Macedonians were eradicated. By 1952 Bulgarian claims on Greek Macedonia were once again being pressed hard. As Bulgarian propaganda intensified, so Greece was pushed closer to Yugoslavia, and Yugoslavia was drawn closer to Greece as her fears of Soviet–Bulgarian–Albanian encirclement mounted. In 1953 a Treaty of Friendship and Co-operation was concluded in Ankara between Greece, Yugoslavia and Turkey, and in 1954 the Treaty was complemented by a Military Alliance signed in Bled.[5]

The dispute over Greek Macedonia continued among the KKE leaders in exile. Zachariades, who had already in 1949 declared his sympathy for the emancipation of the Slavophones, declared unmistakably in his 'Ten Years of Struggle' that he supported the political autonomy and self-government of the Macedonian Slavs, thus making life exceedingly difficult for his fellow Communists in Greece[6]. Because there was an implication in his statement that he favoured a Bulgarian-orientated but independent Macedonia – and not the Yugoslav variety – he was condemned by both Moscow and Sofia. Partsalides, a member of the Central Committee (and a revered figure of the internal KKE after 1960), heavily criticized his leader's separatist pronouncements as reviving a mistake that had plagued the KKE during the inter-war period.

With Stalin's death in 1953, relations between Belgrade and Moscow improved, leading to a Yugoslav–Bulgarian *rapprochement* in 1955. However, the suppression of the Hungarian uprising in 1956 brought about another deterioration, lasting until 1960. In 1959 Greece and Yugoslavia agreed on free border traffic, but this was denounced by Greece in 1962 after renewed hostility over the issue of Macedonia. A new period of understanding between the Soviet Union and Yugoslavia began in 1962, but also foundered – this time as a result of Soviet intervention in Czechoslovakia in 1968.

The see-saw of improvement and deterioration in Yugoslav–Soviet–Bulgarian relations had a marked impact on Greece. Every normalization of relations among the three countries meant that Yugoslavia would revive her accusations that Greece was depriving her alleged Macedonian minority of its cultural heritage. The standard Greek reply amounted to a denial of the existence of such a minority.

From the end of World War II Greece's primary concern over Macedonia was to maintain the territorial *status quo*. It was assumed that occasional Yugoslav statements supporting the rights of the alleged minority in Greece were stimulated by both pressure from Skopje (the centre for Macedonian nationalism) and the need to confront Bulgarian arguments with a principled position on the identity of the Macedonian Slavophones. Greek tactics with respect to such intermittent Yugoslav and Bulgarian claims were to respond to, rather than to initiate, verbal aggression and to try to play down what was considered an artificial issue.

Graeco–Romanian relations from 1957 to 1959 were highlighted by the Stoika Plan to ban nuclear weapons from the Balkans. This Romanian proposition was adopted by the left-wing coalition party EDA and was extensively employed during electoral campaigning.

Improvement of relations between Greece and her Communist neighbours was initiated by the dictatorship in 1967 because the regime was experiencing political if not economic isolation from Western Europe. Bulgaria's favourable response to Greek overtures indicated Soviet willingness to exploit Greek isolation, but it could also be seen in the wider context of global detente. The Soviet intervention in Czechoslovakia had an adverse effect of Tito's relations with Bulgaria, and the Greek Colonels had no desire to alleviate Yugoslavia's problem. Irritated by criticism from Yugoslavia in 1967 over the arrest of political dissidents, the Colonels denounced the 1959 Agreement concerning frontier traffic. Relations with Yugoslavia improved after 1970 on the Greek Government's initiative.[7]

Greece and Albania resumed diplomatic relations in May 1971. These had been severed during the War, and Greek claims on territories and war indemnities were excluded from the negotiations – which were thus about trade and cultural exchanges only.

Since the restoration of democracy in 1974, as a result of the tensions over Cyprus and the Aegean, Greece has consistently pursued a comprehensive Balkan policy to secure her northern frontiers by improving relations with all her Communist neighbours. This *rapprochement* can also be viewed as a necessary and overdue adjustment to bring Greece into the era of detente and Eurocommunism. To quote an apt comment, 'If we were to compare the growth of East–West trade and the volume of scientific and technological exchanges between the industrial West and the developing East with Greece's timid initiatives during the 1960s, we would find that the country's foreign policy was in disharmony even with that of its NATO partners'.[8]

Besides her importance in providing the most accessible land-route to Western Europe, Yugoslavia's influence among the non-aligned countries was considered useful in the Cyprus dispute. Greece and Yugoslavia agreed to relieve their mutual borders of a concentration of troops and to divert them to other areas vital for their respective national defences. Old problems such as the free zone at Thessaloniki were settled, and trade between Greece and Yugoslavia grew from $120 million in 1975 to $250 million in 1980. Greek entry into the European Economic Community (EEC) and restrictions on trade with non-members reduced this figure to $208 million for 1981 and turned the balance in Greece's favour. A pipeline to bring oil from the Aegean to Skopje is being constructed, and goodwill visits were exchanged between Karamanlis and Tito, as well as between other members of their respective Governments. The death of Tito has somewhat numbed the initiative of his successors but has not altered the friendliness of relations between the two nations. Yugoslavia's backing of Skopje's claims over the alleged Macedonian minorities is basically aimed at Bulgaria, but the matter is also of concern to Greece and so causes irritation in Athens. The difference of view however, between the central Yugoslavian Government and 'Macedonian' Skopje is that Skopje considers the recognition of a 'Macedonian minority' a precondition for any further improvement in Yugoslav–Greek relations, whereas the Government in Belgrade believes that friendly relations between Greece and Yugoslavia will also promote a solution to the Macedonian problem. It is logical to assume therefore that any future weakening of Belgrade's control over Skopje will rekindle friction between Greece and Yugoslavia.[9]

Relations with Albania – improving steadily since 1971 – reached a high point after Hoxha's break with China. Visits of a commercial and cultural nature were exchanged starting in 1977, and trade amounting to a total of $21 million was exchanged. A regular air link between Athens and Tirana was inaugurated in 1978. Hoxha himself took a friendly stance towards the Greek minority in his country (estimated by a Western source to amount to anything between 40,000 and

80,000), the status of which constituted the most serious obstacle in any Graeco–Albanian *rapprochement*. Besides stressing the need for closer relations with Greece, the Albanian leader has extolled the importance of preserving Greek language, culture and tradition among the Albanian Greeks.[10]

The opening towards Bulgaria was mainly the result of a personal initiative by Karamanlis and his individual style of conducting foreign policy. After visiting an enthusiastic Nicolae Ceaucescu in Romania in May 1975 and visiting Yugoslavia in June of the same year, he was received by Todar Zhivkov of Bulgaria on 2–3 July. Although Graeco–Bulgarian relations have been troubled in the past, Karamanlis' direct appeal to Zhivkov eventually made an impression on Bulgarian reluctance to enter into a multilateral relationship even on a limited basis. Initially Bulgaria attempted to enlarge Balkan multilateral initiatives to include other East European nations. Following a Greek initiative, however, an inter-Balkan Conference of Deputy Ministers of Planning (or Undersecretaries for Co-ordination) took place in Athens in February 1976. Although Bulgaria opposed Balkan multilateralism in principle, she nevertheless attended the summit to avoid discouraging the two NATO participants – Greece and Turkey – from their dialogue with the East. A renewed effort by Karamanlis to give the Summit Meetings a regular and substantial character was politely rebuffed by Bulgaria, reflecting perhaps Soviet fears that institutionalized Balkan co-operation might adversely affect the cohesion of the Warsaw Pact. That fear may be diminishing. At the April 1979 Corfu meeting with Karamanlis, President Zhivkov appeared to have overcome his inhibitions, and he then agreed to multilateralism in specified fields.[11]

Considering the strains of the past between the two nations, Graeco–Bulgarian relations are now uncommonly good. No territorial or minority claims marred the exchange of visits between Karamanlis and Zhivkov. It can be anticipated that Papandreou's Government will press further. Commerce increased from $104 million in 1978 to a total of $157 million in 1980,[12] while industrial co-operation, the linking of electrical grids, access to the 'free port' of Thessaloniki and the expansion of vital land communications have been agreed.[13]

Despite a generally encouraging trend in Greece's relations with the other Balkan states, the Soviet Union can still threaten to exploit latent discontent among ethnic groups and differences over contested territories. Either or both could destabilize the present delicate balance. The Macedonian dispute, which is now mainly between Yugoslavia and Bulgaria, may return in the 1980s, initiated possibly by Belgrade (to appease Skopjean nationalism) or by Sofia (whose old claims on what is today Yugoslav Macedonia may be encouraged by Moscow to embarrass Yugoslavia). Yugoslav apprehensions, which subsided after Tito's death, were rekindled at the beginning of 1981 when Bulgaria celebrated 1,300 years of statehood.

Her position as an outsider to these quarrels among Communist states has enhanced Greece's credibility as an honest broker in the Balkans. The efforts of Karamanlis were initially blunted by Bulgaria, and Greece was also faced with Turkish fears that a Balkan Pact might contribute to Turkey's isolation. However, most Balkan leaders have taken care not to offend Turkey and, according to Stavrou, even Yugoslavia, 'usually a trustworthy friend of Greece, has had to reconcile any response to a Greek–Turkish dispute with its role in the non-aligned movement and with its national interest'.[14] Greece's major objective in the Balkans has not been to secure allies against Turkey but rather to relieve her own borders from tension in case of any attack from the East.[15]

In short Greece has to a quite satisfactory exent established both bilateral and multilateral relations in the Balkans after decades of mutual distrust. Since his electoral victory, Papandreou has furthered his friendly policy towards Communist Balkan states by receiving Ceaucescu in Athens and visting Belgrade and Sofia.[16]

**Graeco–Turkish Relations**
The favourable trend in Graeco–Turkish relations created by the 1930 Accord and the 1933 and 1938 Treaties of Military Co-

operation was interrupted by the outbreak of World War II. In 1939 Turkey concluded a Trilateral Treaty with Britain and France, undertaking the obligation to 'lend them all aid and assistance' in case any of the signatories was involved in war with a European power in the Mediterranean.[17] Her subsequent failure to enter the war affected Greece badly, since she was under very great pressure from Axis forces. Furthermore, a Turkish capital tax (*varlik vergisi*), which operated between 1942 and 1944, caused considerable hardship to the ethnic minorities of Istanbul, and in particular to Turkish citizens of Greek, Jewish and Armenian origin.[18]

By 1951, however, Greece and Turkey had resumed friendly relations in the face of a common Soviet threat. Both were recipients of aid under the Marshall Plan, and both were formally admitted into NATO on 18 February 1952, at the height of the Cold War. A year later they signed, together with Yugoslavia, a Treaty of Friendship and Cooperation followed by a formal Alliance. The Alliance, which might have served as an indirect link between NATO and Yugoslavia, foundered on the improvement of Russian–Yugoslav relations in 1955 as well as on the Cyprus issue, which for almost a quarter of a century has been the major source of tension between the two NATO allies.

*The Cyprus Problem*
Cyprus was occupied by Britain in 1878 and became a colony in 1925. Her mixed population (80 per cent Greek and 18 per cent Turkish) and her position as an important strategic location in the Eastern Mediterranean meant that the island soon became a bone of contention between states of the Western Alliance. The Greek-Cypriot claim for self-determination in order to unite the island with Greece – a mixture of traditional irredentism and contemporary anti-colonialism – was initially confronted by Britain's reluctance to abandon her position in the Eastern Mediterranean; and later the same mixture served to inflame nationalist feeling in Greece and Turkey, and to erode their respective relations with the United States. NATO became implicated in the dispute in the 1960s. The Organization was designed to provide a defence against the Soviet Union, and it operates on the assumption that the notion of collective security supersedes all other local priorities. It was therefore ill-equipped to resolve local disputes between its members.

In January 1950 a plebiscite of Greek Cypriots was organized by the Orthodox Church. This yielded a 96 per cent vote in favour of unification (*enosis*) with Greece, and revived old pressures on Greece to take up the issue with Britain. Greek Governments since 1931 had carefully avoided claims that would cause friction with Britain, and the Liberal Coalition Government of 1951 was no exception to that rule. Yet the United States was all the while assuming a dominant position in Greece, and in consequence Greek inhibitions towards Britain gradually diminished. In 1954 the Conservative Government of Marshal Papagos, strongly committed to the United States, embraced the cause of the Greek Cypriots.[19]

When Archbishop Makarios, then political and spiritual leader of the Greek-Cypriot community, began to steer the question towards the United Nations, Britain decided to introduce Turkey (hitherto apathetic about the conflict) into the matter, to provide a counter-weight to Greek demands. The Turkish Government assumed responsibility for the welfare of the Turkish Cypriots and eventually control over their affairs. Thus the foundations of the future intercommunal conflict were laid, and what began as an anti-colonial struggle gradually developed into a confrontation between Greek and Turk.

Relations between Greece and Turkey deteriorated in September 1955 when a mob in Istanbul, demanding the annexation of Cyprus by Turkey, attacked and destroyed Greek houses, shops and churches.[20] By 1959 the Cyprus issue had become such a liability for Greece's relations with Britain and the United States that Prime Minister Karamanlis felt compelled to seek a speedy solution to the problem. Makarios in the meantime had retreated from the *enosis* aspiration, for this provoked Turkish demands for the partition of the island. He adopted instead his platform of Cypriot independence. Finally Britain came to realize that to retain control of Cyprus in opposition to the Greek Cypriots was becoming too expensive. She sought a way of reconciling the retention of sovereign base rights with Cypriot independence.

In 1959 the Greek Prime Minister Karamanlis and the Turkish Prime Minister Menderes drafted an agreement in Zurich for the creation of an independent Cyprus. This plan was duly presented to the leaders of the two communities. The agreement provided for the British sovereign military bases in the island and an independent republic for the Cypriots. The integrity and constitution of the state were to be guaranteed by Britain, Greece and Turkey, and the latter two states would contribute contingency forces of 950 and 650 respectively. A Greek-Cypriot President and a Turkish-Cypriot Vice-President were given veto power over vital legislation, and the Turkish minority was represented in the Government and in the Civil Service to a greater extent than numbers demanded. The leaders of the two communities, who had played no part in the drafting of the Zurich Agreement, affixed their signatures to the document in London.

After the electoral defeat of Karamanlis in 1963, the Centre Union coalition under the ageing George Papandreou was faced with a new phase in the Cyprus entanglement – the protracted struggle between the ethnic groups of the island. Confronted with a deadlock in the passing of vital legislation, President Makarios proposed to Dr Kutchuck, the Turkish-Cypriot Vice-President, thirteen amendments to the 1960 Constitution. The veto powers of both the President and (more important to the Turks) the Vice-President would be abolished, and the number of Turkish Cypriots in the Administration would be diminished. Turkey, followed by Dr Kutchuck, rejected the proposals, and fighting broke out between the two communities which lasted well into the Summer of 1964 and caused considerable hardship for the outnumbered Turkish Cypriots. It was only after US President Johnson's personal warning to the Turkish Prime Minister Ismet Inönü that a Turkish invasion of Cyprus was warded off during the Summer. An uneasy peace was restored by a UN peacekeeping force (UNFICYP), but mutual hatred continued to smoulder.

General Grivas, already head of the most active anti-Communist band when the German forces pulled out of Greece, had become leader of the guerrilla EOKA movement in Cyprus which harassed the British forces between 1955 and 1959. A champion of *enosis*, he strongly disapproved of the Zurich Settlement and of Makarios' policy of pursuing independence rather than unification with Greece. In November 1967 Grivas, now commander of the Greek-Cypriot National Guard, attacked Turkish-Cypriot villages, thus provoking a new threat of Turkish invasion. This threat was once again averted by American and NATO intervention, leading to the removal both of excessive Greek forces and of General Grivas from the island. Grivas, however, returned to Cyprus secretly in 1971 and eventually founded the EOKA-B organization, which became an agent of destabilization of the Archbishop's Government and undermined the progress of intercommunal talks.[21]

EOKA-B shared the conviction of the Greek military regime (which took power in 1967) that Makarios, with his alleged Communist sympathies, jeopardized both the prospect of eventual *enosis* as well as the position of the Western Alliance in the Eastern Mediterranean. Furthermore, they believed that *enosis* (with attendant concessions to Turkey) had been blessed by the United States as the best way of bringing the island into NATO, and they also saw *enosis* as a way of getting rid of a neutralist Makarios. It was on the basis of these assumptions that the Greek military regime (Junta) launched the coup against the Archbishop in July 1974 which led to Turkey's occupation of the northern part of the island.

The Junta's interest in Cyprus was believed to run parallel to that of the United States. Turkey, already on bad terms with the Greek Junta because of disputed claims over the Aegean continental shelf, was in no mood to compromise over Cyprus. Furthermore, US–Turkish relations had changed since the Johnson era, with Turkey becoming more assertive. Prior to the coup against Makarios, Ankara had informed Washington that it would not restrict opium production, thus asserting Turkey's interests in the face of American pressure.

Although Turkey did not react to the coup against Makarios immediately, this was soon seen as a golden opportunity to exercise the right of intervention which they argued had been conferred on them by the 1960 Treaty of Guarantee.[22] International detente had considerably reduced the possibility of effective Soviet reaction, and the Junta's choice of an old enemy of the Turkish community, Nicos Sampson, to replace Makarios sealed the fate of the island. In the words of an important Turkish diplomat in Washington, 'The Greeks committed the unbelievably stupid move of appointing Sampson, giving us the opportunity to solve our problems once and for all. Unlike 1964 and 1967, the United States leverage on us in 1974 was minimal. We could no longer be scared off by threats of the Soviet bogeyman'.[23]

American Undersecretary of State Joseph Sisco was sent to Ankara to mediate, but there he met an adamant Prime Minister Ecevit, who, ironically, put forward the very demand that Makarios had put to Athens, namely the removal of the Greek officers serving with the Cyprus National Guard.[24] Ecevit also demanded the establishment of a federal state with Turkish and Greek components with permanent access to the sea to permit forces to intervene. When Sisco conveyed these terms to the military regime in Athens he was confronted with incredulity and confusion. The Junta acted as if they had never anticipated the possibility of a Turkish invasion.

When the Turkish forces landed near Kyrenia, the Junta hastily ordered a chaotic general mobilization, which betrayed the regime's total unpreparedness for such an eventuality. According to an account by a Greek official who had access to classified records of the invasion:

> Even as the Turkish ships were steaming towards the shore, the Greeks had no orders from their commanders to shoot. The national guard was sending messages: 'the ships are coming, there are planes overhead, but we have no orders to fire'. It was only when the Turkish paratroopers began landing over Nicosia that a reaction was ordered by the Greek commanders.[25]

In a matter of days the Junta disintegrated. On 23 July it handed power hastily to a civilian government under Karamanlis – who was summoned back from Paris after an absence of eleven years. Although Turkey had agreed to a cease-fire, she continued to land troops and supplies and extended her control in breach of the agreement. At the conference held in Geneva, Turkey refused to accept the Greek plea for the removal of her forces or, later, to withdraw her advancing troops to the cease-fire line established on 30 June. Two plans were handed over to the Greeks. The Turkish-Cypriot leader, Denktash, asked for a bizonal federation with a demarcation line running across the island through Nicosia and Famagusta, with the northern part for the Turks. The Turkish Foreign Minister, Gunes, submitted a plan for six autonomous Turkish cantons. Both plans involved 34 per cent of Cyprus passing under Turkish-Cypriot rule. A request by the Greek and Greek-Cypriot representatives for thirty-six hours to consult with their Governments was refused by Turkey, and the second phase of her invasion – known as Attila II – was put into effect on 14 August. By 16 August 37 per cent of the island had come under Turkish control and 200,000 Greek Cypriots (roughly a third of the island's population) had been displaced from their homes and had flocked into improvised refugee camps in the southern part of Cyprus.

Since the *status quo ante* had been restored during the first days of the invasion, Attila II had no legal basis or other purpose except to consolidate the position of Turkey on the island.

According to Nancy Crawshaw, 'From now on considerations of strategy took priority over the obligations imposed by the Zurich Treaties, which specifically precluded partition and the division of Cyprus into separate states'.[26] Turkish Cypriots from the South and immigrants from Turkey were settled in the North of the island to fill the vacuum that the flight of the Greek-Cypriot refugees had created.

Following the second Turkish offensive, Karamanlis dispelled any doubt that Greece might come to the rescue of Cyprus. The general shock at what was considered to be NATO's apathy over Turkey's determination to impose her own solution on the island was expressed by the Greek withdrawal from the military arm of the Alliance. Although of questionable strategic good sense, the decision was justified as the only alternative to war with Turkey (for which Greece was quite unprepared). Karamanlis also pointed out the decline in credibility of the Alliance during the preceding seven years.

The only moral consolation for the Greek Cypriots was the UN General Assembly's unanimous Resolution 3212 of November 1974, urging a withdrawal of all foreign troops from Cyprus and the return of all refugees to their homes in safety, as well as the endorsement of this Resolution by the Security Council in December. In April 1975 intercommunal talks were resumed in Vienna under the auspices of UN Secretary General Kurt Waldheim, followed by a meeting between Karamanlis and Turkish Prime Minister Demirel which endorsed the talks. During the third round of talks in Vienna, the Greek-Cypriot negotiator, Glafkos Clerides, agreed to allow the passage of 10,000 Turkish Cypriots to the north, but comprehensive proposals promised by Denktash failed to materialize, and all but 2,000 Greeks were expelled from their homes in the North in spite of an agreement to safeguard their position. At the end of the year the Greek and Turkish Foreign Ministers sought resumption of the intercommunal discussions with the aim of formulating a package deal in an agenda covering territorial matters, the features of a federation and the competence of the central Government. In February 1976 both sides agreed to produce proposals within six weeks. On 6 April Greek-Cypriot territorial and constitutional proposals were submitted to the UN Representative. The Turkish-Cypriot plan of 17 April for bizonal federation, however, included no territorial proposals. By September the discussions reached a dead-end as the Turkish Cypriots refused to commit themselves to further proposals. In January and February 1977 Makarios met Denktash and agreed with him on the guidelines of a settlement. In March the sixth round began in Vienna, with the Greek Cypriots handing in a plan for a two-region federation, leaving 20 per cent of the island under Turkish administration. No Turkish-Cypriot territorial proposals appeared.[27]

On 3 August 1977 Makarios died. In view of the *de facto* partition of Cyprus, some of the critics of the Archbishop's non-aligned policy were compelled to admit that it was only through his diplomatic skill that the territorial integrity of the indefensible island had been preserved for so long. His gravest errors had been his refusal to safeguard the needs of the Turkish-Cypriot minority and his failure to realize in time the implications of detente for the fate of the weaker non-aligned nations. However, his evaluations of Turkish strategy and American priorities in the Mediterranean were vindicated.[28]

At the beginning of 1978 Ecevit's return to power and his favourable disposition towards a speedy solution of the Cyprus issue took into account the US Administration's willingness to link the lifting of an arms embargo imposed on Turkey by Congress with progress in Cyprus. On the initiative of the Turkish Prime Minister, Karamanlis and Ecevit met at Montreux in March 1978 'in order to create a climate of confidence'. In April, however, the US State Department announced its decision to back the lifting of the arms embargo, and the Greek Government was faced with criticism at home for allegedly promoting Turkey's peace-loving image. The long-awaited Turkish-Cypriot proposals, delivered to the UN Secretary General on 13 April, were such a disappointment to the Greek Cypriots that all efforts at finding a solution halted. The British *Guardian* newspaper criticized the proposals as 'the most marginal surrender of land [and] an appallingly weak federal government).[29]

Although there were no signs of a solution to the Cypriot deadlock, the United States lifted the arms embargo on 14 August on the following conditions:

*1)* That the President would provide Congress with regular reports on the progress of a solution in Cyprus;

*2)* That no provocations would be made either in the Aegean or in Cyprus;
*3)* That the balance of military strength as it stood in 1978 be maintained.[30]

On 9 November the UN General Assembly passed a resolution to remove Turkish forces from the island and insisted that the Security Council implement it. On 29 November a 12-point US–Canadian–British 'framework for a Cyprus settlement' was released at the United Nations. The framework was rejected by both sides. In his report to the US Congress of 29 January 1979 President Carter wrote: 'the government of Turkey has taken a constructive attitude towards efforts to bring about a resumption of the intercommunal negotiations'. The Reuter News Agency, however, was not of the same mind on 7 February: 'There is an air of pessimism as sources on both sides admit serious differences remain. At the heart of the problem are conditions which the Turkish-Cypriot leadership has set in return for their agreement to return to the negotiating table'.

Efforts by Dr Waldheim brought about the arrangement of a summit meeting between Kyprianou and Denktash, and an agreement was reached on 19 May towards the resumption of the intercommunal dialogue. The common views of the two sides were incorporated in a joint document. The UN Resolution, which Denktash recognized for the first time, was included with the Makarios–Denktash guidelines as a basis for future negotiations.[31] At the beginning of the Summer of 1979 the talks broke down once more, with the Turkish Cypriots refusing to discuss Varosha (Famagusta) first, as agreed, and insisting on amendments to the 19 May Agreement which introduced new terms to the negotiations. In December 1979 the UN reiterated its previous resolutions and set a deadline for positive development in the intercommunal talks, after which a committee would be sent to the island for mediation. Before the deadline expired furious efforts were made to revive the talks. These bore fruit in September 1980 and averted action by the UN and a new appeal by the Cypriot Government. The talks limped on through 1981 after Denktash proposed that only a limited number of inhabitants of Varosha would return to a section of their town which would remain under Turkish arms. The much-acclaimed Turkish proposals of August 1981, although more comprehensive than those of the past, constituted a poor basis for negotiations. The terms amounted to a 4 per cent territorial concession, an upholding of the Confederate system and restricted freedom of movement. In late February 1982, the new Greek Premier, Andreas Papandreou, paid a state visit to the island and declared his solidarity with the cause of an independent Cyprus and asked for the withdrawal of all foreign troops from the island. He offered to finance a larger UN peace-keeping force on the island.

The entire history of post-1975 intercommunal talks was summed up in a memorandum conveyed by Greek-Cypriot Foreign Minister Rolandis to Dr Waldheim in 1979. According to the document, each time the Greek Cypriots made moves to accommodate a Turkish position, the Turkish side has taken a step back, first from 'federation' to 'federation by evolution' and then to proposals for the creation of two virtually separate states.[32]

Besides the Cyprus issue, three other critical questions have given rise to serious tension between Greece and Turkey: *1)* the Aegean continental shelf; *2)* control of the air traffic over the sea; and *3)* the allocation of operational responsibility of the Aegean and its air-space within the framework of NATO.[33]

*The Continental Shelf*
Concerning the first issue, Turkey considers her continental shelf to be an extension of the Asia Minor land mass into the sea to the west of certain Greek islands, to which she denies possession of a continental shelf. It follows that the islanders can only exploit the sea-bed of their islands within the territorial sea limit of six miles. Greece, while referring to the Geneva Convention which recognizes the right of islands to a continental shelf, also reserves her right (following general world practice) to extend her territorial sea limit to twelve miles. Such a decision would automatically solve the continental-shelf con-

troversy in Greece's favour but would, according to Turkey, constitute a *casus belli* because it would limit Turkish access to international waters.[34] Retreating from an earlier commitment, Turkey has insisted that the question of the continental shelf should be solved through political negotiations between the two interested parties, while Greece, although submitting to negotiations, believes that the dispute necessitates a settlement by international legal arbitration[35]. The advantages of such a solution are obvious. International arbitration will save the politicians of both countries from loss of face and a decision made by the International Court of Justice will be easier to accept.

Throughout the Summer of 1976 the Turkish ship *Sismik* conducted seismic research in areas of the Aegean shelf appertaining to Greek islands. Because of bellicose opposition at home and the danger of an armed confrontation with Turkey, the Greek Government appealed to the UN Security Council and simultaneously sought arbitration unilaterally by the International Court of Justice. The Security Council did not attempt to deal with the substance of the dispute but tried to lessen the tensions by asking both sides to abstain from hostile acts. On 11 September 1976 and 19 December 1978 the International Court indicated its inability to come to a decision on the substance of the Greek application.

Since the 1978 Karamanlis–Ecevit meeting in Montreux, however, tension on this specific issue has considerably declined. Both sides agreed to discuss the problem and to abstain from activities (such as magnetometric studies for discovering oil in disputed areas) which would cause friction between them. Although bilateral discussions have not led to a solution so far, they have at least excluded the possibility of recourse to violence. Turkey continues to reject the median line between the islands and the mainland and insists on her formula of equity, but she has refrained from pressing the continental shelf argument.

*Air Traffic Control*
While refusing to accept an extension of Greece's territorial waters, Turkey points out that the existing six-mile limit should set the standard for Greek air space, which since 1932 has extended four miles beyond the limit of Greek territorial sea. By constantly violating the ten-mile limit of Greek airspace with her fighters, Turkey has since 1974 embarked on the dangerous practice of unilaterally redefining Aegean air-space. This systematic testing of nerves may easily lead to tragedy.

A regional convention of the International Civil Aviation Organization (ICAO) in Paris decided in 1952 that the Aegean controlled air-space (except the band of Turkish national air-space off the coast of Asia Minor) should form part of the Athens Flight Information Region (FIR) for air traffic control purposes. All planes flying west (civil or military) were required to file flight plans and to report positions as they crossed the FIR boundary after leaving the coast of Turkey. Planes coming from the opposite direction were required to report to the control centre in Istanbul as they entered the Turkish FIR. As Andrew Wilson has pointed out: 'To have placed the FIR boundary further to the west would have obliged Greek aircraft to pass through a Turkish zone of control on flights to the Greek islands. To this extent the arrangement was consistent with geography and seems to have worked well for 22 years'.[36] On 6 August 1974 the Turkish Authorities issued NOTAM 714 (notice to ICAO for transmission to air users) demanding that all aircraft reaching the median line of the Aegean report their flight plan to Istanbul. Greece refused to accept this contravention of ICAO rules and, on 14 August 1974, issued NOTAM 1157 declaring the Aegean area of the Athens FIR dangerous because of the threat of conflicting control orders. All international flights in the Aegean between the two countries were suspended. On 22 February 1980 Turkey withdrew her claim to air-traffic rights in the eastern half of the Aegean, and the air corridors were subsequently reopened.

*The NATO Framework*
The third issue concerning operational responsibilities in the Aegean will be treated in the following section in some detail. It will be

15

sufficient here to note that, as far as Turkey is concerned, the matter of restructuring responsibilities in the Aegean is now under consideration. The reintegration of Greece into the military structure of NATO in October 1980 was achieved after Turkey was persuaded to postpone her revisionist claims on the operational *status quo* in the Aegean. The PASOK Government seems resolved not to discuss any modifications which may impinge on the safety of the Greek islands, but Andreas Papandreou, in his interview with the *Financial Times* (24 February 1982), admitted that, as Turkish pressure had diminished since the advent of military rule in Ankara, Greece might perhaps exchange her right to extend her territorial waters for the withdrawal of Turkish objections to the pre-1974 operational responsibilities of Greece. Such operational arrangements that exist within the NATO framework, however, are without international legal status, and if Greece chose to withdraw from the structure or to ignore Turkish demands there is nothing that Turkey could do to impose her claims short of war.[37] The problem is not therefore of a legal but rather of a political nature. Since Greece has chosen to pursue her security interests through her membership of NATO, she will be faced in the coming years with the difficult task of constantly assessing the advantages against the liabilities of her choice. What appears to be clear at this point is that no Greek Government can accept arrangements that would affect the air-space of the Greek islands.

In his September 1979 Harvard speech, George Rallis (then Greek Foreign Minister) expressed his country's fundamental concern over the Aegean problem in the following terms: 'Claims that could result in the enclavement of the Greek islands of the Eastern Aegean in a Turkish continental shelf and in a Turkish controlled air-space are obviously unacceptable to Greece, all the more so since such claims have no basis either in International Law or in International practice'.[38]

**Greek Relations with the US and NATO**
Victory against the Communist forces in the Greek civil war was secured through American aid and commitment. The war-ravaged country was not only made safe for the western democratic system but was also given vital transfusions of economic support. A large section of the population considered the Marshall Plan to be manna from heaven and American generosity the epitome of benevolence and altruism. There were, however, three points which invited American penetration of the Greek policy-making process: strategic concern over a Soviet and Balkan threat; the sorely needed economic aid to finance reconstruction; and the political weight that American approval carried in the 1950s. Such approval, whether of a party or a government, carried with it the active promise of support and the passive guarantee of a term in office unobstructed by foreign interference. The mythology of American omnipresence as well as the perpetuation of the Communist scare, which Cold-war politics, eager politicians, administrators and officers encouraged, explain some of the effectiveness of American influence in Greek affairs.[39]

Between 1947 and 1950 American foreign policy in Greece favoured centrist rather than conservative political formations and leaders. This policy was based on the assumption that Greece could face the Communist threat best if social reforms were promoted. In the 1950s, however, the United States became convinced by the Korean War 'that the danger of Soviet expansion was strictly a military one, and that it could be resisted not by political and economic reforms achieved through the democratic left and centre, but by reliance on military elements not merely in strictly military matters but in politics as well'.[40] Ambassador Peurifoy's involvement in Greek politics was so direct that few had doubts in 1951–2 as to which party the Americans favoured. Through his influence, the life of the centre-coalition Government under General Plastiras was shortened, and the simple majority system, endorsed by Peurifoy as a guarantee of stability, facilitated the electoral success of Marshal Papagos (Commander-in-Chief of the Government forces in the civil war), whose conservative party secured some 80 per cent of the seats in Parliament with 49 per cent of the vote. Papagos' success perhaps proved somewhat greater than the Ambassador had anticipated. Staunch in his friendship towards the United States and his anti-Communist sentiments, he was also a nationalist, and he pursued the unification of Cyprus with Greece in spite of the damage it caused in his relations with the other NATO members. Although it is alleged that Papagos' unification policy was not initially opposed by the United States, his stature within the conservative camp made him less manoeuvrable than his weak predecessors. His successor, Constantine Karamanlis, was more concerned with maintaining good relations with NATO and the United States than with pursuing an independent course over the Cyprus issue. American influence, although not American popularity, did not diminish during or after Papagos' term in office. Decisions concerning the economy, the armed forces and the gendarmerie were profoundly affected by American advice and instruction. The reduction or termination of aid and the refusal of loans to correct disequilibria could bring pressure to bear on rare occasions of Greek obstinacy.

The difference between conservatives and liberals on security issues and NATO was one of degree rather than kind. Both sides basically agreed that Greece's main security lay in her northern borders, that Communism threatened mutually cherished values, that NATO was indispensible for the defence of the country and that America was Greece's natural ally and guarantor. The 1953 Greek–American Agreement to provide bases and other facilities for the United States within the framework of NATO was, in general terms, accepted not only by the conservatives but by the more prominent liberals as well. The latter only registered their opposition to the high level of military expenditure and, in 1958, to the installation of American nuclear weapons on Greek soil. They agreed that concessions on that issue could be made in a package deal which would include a favourable settlement of the Cyprus question, or if all other NATO members accepted nuclear bases on their own soil.[41]

The issue which posed the greatest threat to the association of Greece with NATO was that of Cyprus. It has been pointed out that the discussions of the 1956–8 and 1963–4 periods illustrate 'the significantly leftward changes in the positions of the non-Communist political movements in Greece generated by this dispute'.[42] The conservative Government strove unsuccessfully to secure self-determination for the island through the UN. The cool or negative reaction of most NATO members to the Greek cause came as a blow to the conservatives – who were then faced with the predicament of deciding the relative priorities of Greek national aspirations and their dedication to the Western Alliance. The latter prevailed in determining the Government's ultimate disposition towards a speedy settlement in 1959, but NATO lost its initial attraction even to the conservatives, let alone the liberals. The Centre Union exhibited its full support for Cypriot independence after the conclusion of the Zurich–London Agreements. George Papandreou, in line with Makarios, made it his Party's policy to reject NATO involvement in Cypriot affairs and favoured arbitration by the General Assembly of the UN over the crisis that flared in 1963–4. American officials were clearly not pleased.

The exclusive relations between the Americans in Greece and the ruling conservative party throughout the 1950s and early 1960s estranged them from liberal politicians waiting in the wings. The rise of the Centre Union Coalition under George Papandreou coincided with President Kennedy's policy for reform as a deterrent to Communist influence. Although lacking in precision, Papandreou's platform for 'democratization' was charged with the rising expectations of a Greek society experiencing a significant improvement of its standard of living in the early 1960s.[43] Implicit in the notion of 'democratization' was a promise of autonomy in the conduct of Greek foreign policy. Henry Labouisse, Kennedy's Ambassador to Greece, was a choice in keeping with the US Administration's progressive ideas, but he could not dispel the growing strains between American officials in Greece and the Centre Union Government. When the son of George Papandreou, Andreas, attempted as Minister to the Prime Minister, to check CIA and USIA activities in Greece, the Government's relations with the United

17

States deteriorated even further. The Cyprus dispute, however, became the most serious source of mutual irritation. According to Maurice Goldbloom (Labour Information Officer at the US Economic Mission in Greece 1950–51), 'From the American point of view, the crucial thing about the quarrel was not the rights and wrongs of the two communities on the island, but the damage it did to relations between Greece and Turkey, both allies of the United States'.[44]

This quarrel furthermore acquired a special significance for the US position in the Eastern Mediterranean when President Makarios joined the non-aligned movement, a policy which required the maintenance of good relations with potential enemies of the United States. Seizing the opportunity, the Soviet Union declared her support for the integrity of the island and, in 1964, issued warnings that she would not remain passive in case of foreign intervention. Bringing Cyprus under the NATO umbrella by way of *enosis* with elements of partition became, therefore, an option of American policy in 1964. According to the Acheson Plan, the island would be united with Greece; Turkey would acquire a sovereign military base; two Turkish cantons would be formed, exercising local autonomy; and the Greek island of Kastellorizo would be given to Turkey. This plan was rejected by both Greeks and Turks, but the die-hards of *enosis* on the one hand and of partition on the other drew their separate conclusions about American designs on the island – conclusions which precipitated the developments of 1974.

Identification with the right-wing and the throne after 1965 limited the flexibility and scope of American policy in Greece. Throughout the conflict between Papandreou and the King over what the latter felt was a struggle for the control of the armed forces, American officials could not conceal their anxiety over the future of the Monarchy. The coup of 21 April 1967, which averted a likely Papandreou victory at the impending election, was greeted with mixed feelings by the United States, including a certain amount of relief. The Colonels, who had staged the coup over the heads of their superior officers, were extreme right-wingers who had, in the early 1950s, identified with Papagos in his quarrels with the throne. Their credentials included little else besides skills in matters of intelligence and propaganda, and the instant justification of the coup was apparently its mission to prevent a (fictitious) Communist takeover.

The Junta went out of its way to encourage the allegations of American complicity, thus assuming the legitimacy that partnership with the United States provided. Although there was no concrete evidence to support these claims, it was true that the US had not denounced the regime and limited her options even further by dissuading King Constantine from attempting to dismiss the Colonels at the outset. No dilemma over recognition arose since the Ambassador was accredited to the King, and, when the latter fled Greece after a belated attempt to overthrow the Junta in December 1967, normal relations of the US Embassy were continued with the Regent.

The tedium of rationalizations and false hopes employed by American policy-makers to justify their attitude towards the Junta disappointed many of those parliamentarians in Greece who favoured the United States and who had hoped that the US Administration would see through the inherent limitations, let alone the brutalities, of the unpopular regime. An embargo on heavy weapons (although not spare parts) imposed on Greece in April 1967 was suspended in October 1968 following the strain that the Soviet invasion of Czechoslovakia caused in the Balkans. It was re-imposed briefly in the early days of the Nixon Administration. Members of Congress, as well as high-ranking officials, made negative appraisals of the regime's value to the United States; yet the Administration chose to formulate the ambiguous dilemma of 'how to deal with an ally with whose internal order we disagree yet who is a loyal NATO partner.'[45] In fact the dilemma did not exist. Since no possible parliamentary alternative in Greece would have upset the *status quo* in Greek–American relations, America's credibility suffered a steep decline – especially after the National Security Council in 1970, under the direction of Henry Kissinger, advised restoration of full-scale military assistance to the dictatorship. Such official visits to Greece as those by Commander of NATO forces General Goodpaster, Secretary of Defense Melvin Laird, Secretary of State William Rogers, the President's brother Donald Nixon, Secretary of Commerce Maurice Stans and, finally, Vice-President Spiro Agnew, did more for the regime than any lifting of the embargo.[46]

In the case of short-term gains, the United States relationship with the Colonels was rewarding. American bases in Greece and Greek territory and air-space remained available to the US during the June 1967 War and the September 1970 crisis in Jordan. In 1971–3 the Nixon Administration negotiated important home-porting privileges for the US Sixth Fleet in the Piraeus and Elefsis area. Papadopoulos – the initial strongman of the Junta – not only displayed his loyalty to NATO but also held secret talks on the Cyprus question with Turkey and tried to bring the 'renegade' Archbishop into line. Failing that, the Junta then orchestrated a series of abortive attempts against Makarios' life. With respect to Cyprus, the Colonels combined the irredentist line of Papagos with the conviction that the United States was willing to bring the island into the fold of NATO and to remove Makarios' dangerous influence by supporting its unification with Greece.[47] The Junta felt that the obvious price for such a prize was the removal of Makarios – an all too happy prospect for Ioannides (who had overthrown Papadopoulos in November 1973) who shared American fears of the Archbishop's initiative towards Moscow but was mainly enraged over his alienation from the principle of *enosis*. Far from being the 'Castro of the Mediterranean', Makarios was a political conservative and a traditionalist, practising tactics of balance-of-power diplomacy to avoid partition of Cyprus – an eventuality which ultimately he was unable to forestall.[48]

Interpretations of the developments in Athens during the crisis of July 1974 are based on educated guesswork and logical deduction rather than on confirmed evidence. Ioannides' supporters claimed that their leader had assurances through the CIA that Turkey would welcome Makarios' removal and that intervention would be averted if the rights of the Turkish minority were guaranteed. Some attributed the subsequent disaster to Makarios' escape; others add American duplicity to the interpretation.[49]

Once the Turkish troops had landed on the island, Ioannides gave the Greek Armed Forces orders to counter-attack, but he was faced with the reluctance of his superiors in military rank to follow orders. Given the state of the Greek forces after seven years of mismanagement and the purges of able officers, the decision of the Generals to summon the politicians and seek an armistice appeared to be the most sensible course of action. There were allegations, however, that the American intelligence establishment in Athens – who wanted at all costs to avoid a war between Greece and Turkey – was encouraging the Generals to revolt against Ioannides. His collapse was precipitated by an ultimatum from General Davos, Commander of the Third Army Corps in Macedonia. Be that as it may, the problems of Greece received scant American attention throughout the period of the Colonels' rule and a surprising lack of attention on the eve of the events of July 1974. In May 1974 the Greek-Cypriot and Turkish policy desks were transferred from the office of Near East Affairs to the Office of European Affairs – an office which apparently possessed little experience in Eastern Mediterranean problems. Secretary Kissinger's alleged inaction during the crisis – attributed to his concerns with major developments within the United States – was interupted only in one instance. On 23 July 'strong representations were made with the Colonels in Athens . . . with respect to a possible counter-offensive against Turkey in Thrace.'[50]

Kissinger maintained guarded optimism over the outcome of the discussions in Geneva, even though the terms of the cease-fire agreement were constantly being violated, and he failed to support British efforts at conciliation. It was becoming increasingly obvious that the United States was prepared to let events run their course in Cyprus, and that she would only assume an active role if the two NATO allies were actually at war. After the Turkish invasion the fate of Cyprus had been sealed and, to the United States, partition emerged as the only credible solution.[51] Constant involvement and intervention had characterized US relationships with others for at least twenty-eight years, so that abstention from action could only be viewed as an equally potent instrument of foreign policy. Greece responded by withdrawing from the military branch of NATO and cancelling the home-porting rights of the US Sixth Fleet.

When the United States arms embargo on Turkey came into force in February 1975 after a heated battle between members of Congress and the Ford Administration, Kissinger saw it as Congressional intrusion into his realm of making foreign policy. He attacked the punitive legislation for being a product of a 'Greek lobby' in the United States and implied that the strings were being pulled by the Foreign Ministry in Athens. These claims notwithstanding, the author had ample opportunity throughout the embargo's duration to observe the total disinclination of the Greek Foreign Ministry and Government to involve itself in what was considered to be an internal American affair. The mood of Congress against the Secretary of State had already been shaped, it appeared, by his record in Chile, by the war in Vietnam and Cambodia and by his position *vis-à-vis* the Greek Junta. However, the Congressional backlash can best be explained by post-Watergate hostility towards the President and determination to assert the authority of Congress against the Administration by upholding US Law, i.e., the Foreign Assistance Act of 1961 and the bilateral agreements of 1947 and 1960 between Turkey and the United States.[52]

On 27 March 1976 the United States Administration signed a Defence Cooperation Agreement (DCA) with Turkey providing about one billion dollars worth of military aid over four years in return for the use of 26 installations on Turkish soil. The document rekindled the Greek Government's fears that the military balance with Turkey would be upset in favour of the latter, and the Greek Foreign Minister was quick to initial an Agreement with the United States for military aid to the value of $700 million over four years in return for facilities at four NATO/US bases whose legal status was being renegotiated. The Agreement was never implemented because the DCA with Turkey failed to go into effect; but it did establish the 7:10 ratio by value of military aid which the Greeks hold dear.

Although both the Turkish and the compensatory Greek Agreements were subject to Congressional ratification, Karamanlis was criticized by the opposition, which chose to interpret his action as indirect approval of US military aid to Turkey. On 6 October 1976 the renegotiation of some forty earlier bilateral agreements with respect to the American and NATO military presence in Greece was concluded, but the ratification was witheld pending US negotiations of similar matters in Turkey – and Greece's return to NATO. The new agreement provided that the Suda Bay and Iraklion bases in Crete, the Hellenikon air base and the Nea Makri base near Athens would acquire a Greek commander, and Greek permission would be required for their operation in time of war. As noted earlier, the two bases in Crete are of particular concern to NATO because they facilitate monitoring of Soviet activity in the Eastern Mediterranean as well as storage for the sea mines and nuclear warheads.

President Carter's promises of justice for Cyprus had raised Greek hopes that an equitable solution would be promoted by the new Administration after 1977. American popularity in Greece improved markedly during the first months of the new Administration, but the subsequent efforts of the President to lift the embargo without any substantial evidence of improvement of the situation in Cyprus was seen by the Greeks as yet another display of American *realpolitik* – in which Greek concerns had a low priority.

Ironically it was her anxiety over what she perceived as the threat from a NATO ally, and not the original *raison d'être* of NATO (i.e., the Soviet danger), which compelled the Greek Government in June 1977 to table a proposition for a special military relationship with the Atlantic Alliance. The proposition involved the reintegration of the Greek Armed Forces into the Alliance in case of an East–West conflict, together with the establishment at Larissa of a regional NATO headquarters under Greek command. On matters of operational responsibilities in the Aegean, Greece asked for a return to the *status quo ante* (i.e., before her 1974 withdrawal from the integrated military structure). An understanding along those lines was reached in February 1978 between the Supreme Commander of NATO (then General Haig) and the Commander-in-Chief of the Greek Armed Forces, General Davos, which was accepted by all NATO members except Turkey.

However, a second formula appeared in Greek newspapers in May 1979. This caused embarrassment to the Greek Government which was accused by the opposition of negotiating vital issues of national defence in complete secrecy. The new set of proposals, which General Haig produced after consulting Turkish officials, included articles which revised the *status quo ante* 1974. The points criticized by the Greek press can be summarized as follows: Greece would forfeit operational responsibility over the air-space of her eastern islands; the Larissa Headquarters determining questions of Aegean defence would be placed under NATO command; and areas of the Aegean sea vital for Greek security would be entrusted to the care of an *ad hoc* NATO task force. This set of proposals was promptly rejected by the Greek Chief of the General Staff, and this was followed by Haig's final proposals as SACEUR, including a plan to commit responsibility for the largest part of the Aegean to a NATO commander. The November 1979 proposals by General Rogers (who became SACEUR in June 1979) attempted to reduce the problem of Greek re-entry into a Graeco–Turkish dispute.

Although it was through SACEUR's decision in 1964 that the operational responsibility for the Aegean air-space assigned to Greece would coincide with her FIR, the Haig and Rogers Plans were justified on the basis that changes had taken place since 1974 which posed obstacles to a return to the *status quo ante* concerning Greek and Turkish areas of operational control. It is therefore necessary to examine these changes in order to verify the basis of such a claim.

Until 1974, an American COMLANDSOUTH-EAST (Commander Allied Land Forces South Eastern Europe), based at Izmir, had co-ordinated both Greek and Turkish land forces – each possessing operational responsibility within its sovereign territory. An American COMSIXATAF (Commander 6th Allied Tactical Air Force), also based in Izmir and subordinate to COMAIRSOUTH in Naples, co-ordinated Greek and Turkish Air Forces, each maintaining responsibility within the zones coinciding with the outer limits of their sovereign air spaces. Pending Greek re-entry into the military command of NATO, the two Izmir HQs were reconstructed to operate under Turkish command while separate headquarters were to be set up in Greece (in Larissa) under Greek command.

The reconsideration of operational responsibilities did not appear to many Greeks to be the logical outcome of the separation of commands. In other words, the fact that Greeks and Turks could not continue to operate in joint headquarters did not necessarily entail a restructuring of zones of operational responsibilities. Turkey argues that she had in fact sought a revision of the operational *status quo* prior to 1974 and that she had registered with NATO her opposition to the 1957 and 1964 decisions. Her demands therefore (as reflected in the Haig and Rogers proposals) focus on a westward extension of her Air Force's operational responsibility over an Aegean archipelago studded with Greek islands, and they do not appear to be matters to be resolved between Greece and Turkey. General Rogers, however, implied during the discussion of his November 1979 proposals with General Davos that Greece and Turkey should examine bilaterally the issue.

With respect to Naval Forces, until 1974 COMEDEAST (Commander Eastern Mediterranean) was – according to the 1957 NATO decision – the Greek Chief of General Naval Staff. COMEDNOREAST (Commander Northeast Mediterranean, covering Turkish territorial waters and the Black Sea) was a Turkish Admiral based in Ankara. Both Commands were subordinate to COMNAVSOUTH (Commander Allied Naval Forces Southern Europe) and ultimately to CINCSOUTH (Commander-in-Chief Allied Forces Southern Europe) in Naples and were not connected with whatever changes occurred in the Izmir

21

land and air headquarters of NATO. After Greek reintegration, the Command of the Eastern Mediterranean should therefore revert automatically to its pre-1974 status.

The question of the future status of the American military bases in Greece, established under the terms of a bilateral agreement signed by the United States and Greece in 1953, is probably one of the most sensitive to be faced by the Papandreou Government. Having originally promised to dismantle the installations, the new Premier is now considering the practical aspects of such a decision. The bases, and particularly the ones in Crete, have been a subject of heated debate since the Cyprus crisis of 1974, because many Greeks believe that they played a role in Turkey's seizure of northern Cyprus. Furthermore, an investigation published in the daily *To Vima* in the Autumn of 1981, suggested that Herakleion and Hellenikon also have a strategic role by helping to determine the complex flight patterns followed by the fleet of strategic nuclear bombers the US Air Force keeps airborne at all times. The report also indicated that, in the event of war, Herakleion can be used, in co-operation with other bases, to fix a target and direct nuclear missiles against it. These activities, the report suggested, could make the bases likely targets for nuclear retaliation. If the bases are dismantled, however, Papandreou must face the cost of replacing through Greece's own means an infrastructure worth hundreds of millions of dollars, as well as the relative strengthening of Turkey's position in NATO.[53]

There has been no conclusion to date of the discussions concerning the US–Greek Defense Co-operation Agreement (defining the status and operation of US bases on Greek soil) which was initialled in July 1977. The deadlock in the negotiations dates from mid-June 1981 and was due to American refusal to accept some of the more important Greek demands. These include the amount of military aid and weapons systems required by Greece, a US guarantee that the 7:10 ratio between Greece and Turkey in terms of arms supply will be maintained in future, a guarantee that no act of armed aggression between the two will be tolerated, and – more important for the US – the demand that the terms which govern the operation of the bases under joint control should include the prerogative of the Greek Government to limit or suspend their activities under special circumstances.[54]

The victory of PASOK in the elections of October 1981 appeared to alter the basis of negotiations. The new Prime Minister asked the United States to guarantee Greek security against an attack from Turkey, since NATO was prevented by the Turkish veto from considering such a demand. The discussions on the future of the bases, however, are not encouraged by circumstances. PASOK cannot bring itself to admit to its public the vagaries of international politics nor to face the fact that the US has become a tougher negotiator. The Americans, on the other hand, do not appear to be in a hurry to reach a new agreement, since the bases continue to operate under favourable terms.

By May 1982 the Greek Premier initiated an opening towards the West, accentuated by a corresponding deterioration of relationships between PASOK and the Moscow-orientated KKE. Greek ratification of Spanish entry into NATO, Secretary Haig's visit to Athens and Greek willingness to participate in a NATO exercise led by a Turkish Commander constituted the highlights of this impressive change of stance. Concerning the status of the bases, examined in October, Papandreou appears to insist on three demands: the preservation of the balance of power in the Aegean; an 'adequate contribution' to Greece's military needs; and control of operations so that the bases might not be used against friendly countries.[55] Violations of Greek air-space on 26 May by Turkish fighters obliged Greece to withdraw her forces from the NATO *Deterrent Force 82* naval exercise in the Eastern Mediterranean and to file strong protests with Turkey and NATO. Turkey refused to accept the Greek *démarche*, stating that she did not recognize the ten-mile limit of Greek air-space, and she simultaneously declared her intention to extend the limit of Turkish territorial sea beyond six miles.[56] This development may have served as a reminder to the Greek Prime Minister that Turkey was still able to call the tune in the Aegean.

## III. DOMESTIC FACTORS

### PASOK

The elections of 19 October 1981 gave a Socialist party an absolute majority of seats in Parliament for the first time in Greek history. The Panhellenic Socialist Movement (PASOK) under the leadership of Andreas Papandreou had made great strides, winning 13.5 per cent of the votes in 1974, 25.3 per cent and 48.1 per cent (with 172 deputies in Parliament) in 1981. The party's leader, the charismatic Andreas (as he is widely known) commands unquestioned authority over a compliant party apparatus, and he personally determines most of its activities. PASOK was founded in 1974 as a continuation of his Panhellenic Liberation Movement, which operated during the Junta period, and, unlike most traditional Greek political formations with the exception of the Communist Party, it has become a mass party with a formidable grass-roots organization and regional committees, relying on influential professionals rather than on local bosses and patrons for its regional representation.

A former Berkeley professor of economics, Andreas Papandreou has in the past drawn on his American experience to criticize the United States in terms which often sounded deliberately simplistic. In doing so, however, he has effectively capitalized on the ill-feeling generated in Greece by American foreign policy during the Junta period and the Cyprus crisis.

National independence, popular sovereignty and social liberation constitute the main points of PASOK's ideology – which has been described as populist leftist, combining national pride with faith in the people's infallibility. In spite of its claims to Marxist authenticity – which, incidentally, have not been reiterated after the elections – the party extends its appeal to the disaffected of all social classes and holds a promise for every Greek except the agents of 'foreign imperialism'. In practical terms PASOK draws the bulk of its constitutents from those who feel that they have missed out on the development boom of the late 1960s and 1970s. Although the Greek farmer of today has little in common with his isolated and impoverished counterpart of the past, PASOK has successfully exploited the grievances of the peasants and those who have crowded into the cities.

The realization of popular sovereignty and social liberation, depends, according to PASOK, on the achievement of national independence, since the relation between these three fundamental goals is seen as a 'linear succession of stages'.[1] The party's most important source of political capital stems directly from the resentment that the average Greek feels against dependence on Great Powers. According to Papandreou, Greece belongs to the Third-world periphery which is exploited by the capitalists of Western Europe and the United States. Critical of the United States for sharing world domination with the Soviet Union, he is an exponent of non-alignment on the model of Yugoslavia and certain Arab states. In his evaluation of detente, peaceful co-existence and the post-Helsinki 'competitive co-existence' between the super-powers, he claims that the initiative has always been with the US because it is in the nature of capitalism to expand or perish. Thus it is the contraction of profit margins which has led the US to greater exploitation of the Third World, and to search for investments in the USSR and China.[2]

According to Papandreou, the Middle East and the Persian Gulf occupy a top position on America's list of priorities because of her need for Arab oil to supplement her own production. Makarios' neutralism and Arab connections, as well as the proximity of Cyprus to Israel, have been a source of constant US anxiety. The incorporation of the island into NATO, either through unification with Greece (an option of the past) or through domination by Turkey (a post-1974 option), has been a US imperative since the late 1950s. The malleability of the Greek Junta and its oafish foreign policy paved the way for the ultimate 'solution' of the Cyprus problem.

Andreas Papandreou rejects the evolutionary tactics of Social Democracy and considers Western tolerance of Euro-communism as an effort of the industrial north to pacify its own working class. He calls on all 'non-aligned' Mediterranean countries to join forces against great-power influence, and he maintains that Greece should pursue her own self-interest and disassociate herself from foreign patrons. He considers Turkey and Israel to be the two pillars of American policy in the Middle East, and he expects Greece to stand no chance in competition with Turkey either in the bilateral context with the US or in NATO if Turkey persists with her demands in the Aegean. He argues that the Turkish barrage of claims are aimed at subverting Greek sovereignty over the islands close to Asia Minor. With a Turkish continental shelf that will encircle these islands, and foreign control of their air-space, either their populations will be forced to abandon them or else Turkey will raise her old contention that Greece is not capable of defending them effectively. Papandreou has accused the previous New Democracy Government of conducting discussions and negotiations that would have compromised sovereign Greek rights, and he has pointed out that since Turkey makes these claims she should appeal to the International Courts for arbitration.[3]

During his electoral campaign in 1981 Papandreou played down his opposition to the EEC and promised to submit the question of membership to a plebiscite. His shift towards legitimacy was accentuated by PASOK's invitation to European Socialist Party leaders to gather in Corfu during the Summer of 1980, there to discuss problems of socialism. Since most of the leaders present did not oppose either the EEC or NATO, Papandreou appeared by implication to have reconciled his party with Greece's dual membership. The rift between the more radical Executive Bureau of the party and its moderate parliamentary representatives has underlined the party's predicament – caught between radical purism on the one hand and the need to modify its position to gain wider support among liberal and even conservative sectors of the electorate on the other. Throughout the Winter and Spring of 1981 Papandreou had conducted a low-key campaign against the Government, hoping perhaps to reconcile PASOK to a constituency disappointed by the performance of the ruling party but which was still sensitive to the possibility of social upheaval.

Papandreou's interview to the daily *To Vima* on 26 April 1981 sparked off a debate which may well continue. PASOK's leader covered the most important domestic and foreign policy issues in this interview. He distinguished between 'socialization' as advocated by PASOK and 'nationalization', which he thought was already excessive and inefficiently carried out by state employees. 'Socialization' would involve state encouragement to agricultural co-operatives and an extension of bank credit to competitive firms and to those that provided services to society and control of the key industries. Concerning defence and foreign policy issues, Papandreou maintained that Greece had the capital and knowledge to set up an advanced arms industry, that he would seek the removal of all nuclear weapons from the country and discourage participation in 'cold war blocs'.

On the timing of withdrawal from NATO, Papandreou promised to take into account the country's need for military equipment as well as the existing balance of power in the world (especially in the Balkan region). He also insisted that as long as US bases remained in operation they would have to be under effective Greek control. Their future would depend on American willingness to supply the Greek armed forces under terms as favourable as those granted to Turkey.

Finally, he dismissed suggestions that PASOK's ultimate objectives had changed since the party was established in 1974. 'A party which is close to assuming or has assumed power', he said, 'has several intermediate objectives which are not determined only by its ultimate goals, but also by the strength of the prevailing winds'.[4]

On 20 October 1981 he gave an interview to the American ABC network in which, as the new Prime Minister, he gained the esteem of large sections of the Greek public. Both political friends and enemies welcomed his candid appreciation of Greece's position with respect to the West and Turkey. By identifying Greece's primary security consideration as Turkey, he respected public opinion on that issue, but he also thereby created a significant diversion of attention from the economic problems faced by his Government. His subsequent performance in the November

1981 EEC meeting in London, and in the early December NATO meeting of Defence Ministers in Brussels (Papandreou had retained the defence portfolio), irritated some of his Western colleagues, but on the whole it drew praise at home. Less popular, however, was the Government's reluctance to take a firm position against the military coup in Poland and against the role of the Soviet Union in its perpetration. A timid official amendment came somewhat too late to be convincing.

Papandreou's most substantial departure from his predecessors' line was his opening towards Iraq and the Palestine Liberation Organization (PLO). His refusal to endorse the despatch of an EEC peace force to the Sinai in November, the welcome afforded to Yasser Arafat on his December visit to Athens, and Greece's February 1982 vote in the UN against Israel's annexation of the Golan Heights, signify an altogether new Greek stance with respect to the Middle East. Most recently, Libya's President Gaddafi was invited to Athens, and Arafat visited Greece immediately after his expulsion from Beirut.

**The New Democracy Party**
The 'New Democracy' Party can trace its origins with little effort. General Papagos' right-wing Greek Rally and its subsequent offshoot, the National Radical Union under Constantine Karamanlis, practically shaped political life in post-war Greece. After the fall of the military dictatorship, Karamanlis, heading New Democracy, won both the 1974 and 1977 elections with 54.3 per cent and 41.8 per cent of the vote, respectively. In May 1980 he was elected President of the Republic by parliament and was replaced as head of the Party and as Premier by George Rallis. The latter was the more moderate of the two candidates for succession, the more conservative candidate being the Defence Minister, Evangelos Averof. This orderly change of leadership, effected through the party mechanism without rupturing its ranks, is quite unusual in Greek party politics and can be seen as a further step towards Westernization, pursued by the Administration since 1974.

Karamanlis' own political transformation following his defeat and departure from politics in 1963, have determined New Democracy's general orientation. A staunch anti-Communist and a strong supporter of NATO in the 1950s and early 1960s (although he had considerable personal admiration for De Gaulle), he has, since his triumphant return in 1974, reflected accurately the change of mood in his public. In terms of policy, this has implied the following: a shift of emphasis from loyalty to the United States and NATO to closer ties with Western Europe and the EEC; improvement of relations with the Communist Balkans and the Soviet Union; and greater tolerance of parliamentary and press opposition, highlighted by the 1974 legalization of the Greek Communist Party. More than two decades of consistent anti-Communism without a serious corresponding challenge to Greek internal or external security, has desensitized the public to invocation of the 'red peril'. A feature of this new state of affairs is the eclipse of anti-Communism, not as a political position but as a repressive, all-encompassing state ideology.

Between 1974 and 1980 foreign policy formulation was the exclusive prerogative of Karamanlis, aided by hand-picked professional diplomats. He took pride in the consistency of his policy, and his yearly evaluations of security issues in Parliament differed only marginally. Entry into the European Community, realized in January 1981 after tortuous negotiations, was the hallmark of his dogged pursuit of an 'organic Greek presence in the West'. A guarantee of parliamentary democracy and a peaceful deterrent to counter Turkish intransigence were, in his estimation, the most important by-products of membership of the EEC. His Balkan multilateralism and his 1979 trip to Moscow were to a great extent motivated by concern over Turkey. His own solution to some of the problems between Greece and Turkey includes mutual submission to international legal arbitration, while on the issue of operational responsibility in the Aegean – a matter to be settled between NATO members – he has held steadfastly to the position of upholding the *status quo ante* 1974.[5] Although he claimed that Greece had no choice in 1974 but to assume full control of her armed forces, he recognized the value of

NATO and pursued Greek re-entry so as to avoid the isolation of Greece when Greek sovereign rights were threatened. Karamanlis also acknowledged the importance of sustaining friendship with the US, and he insisted that facilities for the United States in Greece should be governed by considerations of mutual advantage.

The change of leadership in New Democracy and in the Government in 1980 did not alter the principles of foreign policy set by Karamanlis, but the mechanism of implementation changed significantly. Joint sessions between the Prime Minister, the Minister of Defence and the Foreign Minister became instrumental in decision-making. The new Foreign Minister, C. Mitsotakis, initiated an opening towards Turkey which bore – in public estimation at least – his personal stamp. After April 1981 this opening foundered on what were widely regarded in Greece as hostile Turkish acts.

In spite of New Democracy's efforts to modernize its stance from paternalistic conservatism to moderate liberalism, the last elections proved that PASOK was the more successful of the two in seeking out the uncommitted centre vote. The association of New Democracy's political predecessors with the side that won the Civil War not only secured them the conservative and nationalist vote but also the support of those who were afraid to antagonize the state. Ruling party and state went hand in hand, and it was New Democracy's own repudiation of repressive measures against urban and rural opposition groups that in fact encouraged more voters to try their luck with PASOK. Furthermore, the latter's nationalist platform outflanked New Democracy's position as the sole guardian of nationalist orthodoxy.

The electoral defeat of October 1981 – although in no sense abject since the party won 35.9 per cent of the vote – generated a minor panic in its ranks which led to another change of leadership. The choice of Averof as Party leader may add zest to the performance of the major opposition party but it may also impede its efforts to win back the more liberal of its voters who deserted to PASOK. The overall performance of New Democracy in opposition has so far been unimpressive.

### The Centre Union Party

The Centre Union Party was reconstituted in 1974 by former deputies who had supported George Papandreou during his 1965 conflict with the Palace, and a coalition of social democrats and resistance fighters against the Junta. The Centre Union–New Forces combination entered the election of 1974 with the reputation of possessing candidates of the highest calibre, but the overwhelming presence of Karamanlis in the New Democracy Party limited the Centre Union–New Forces to 20.42 per cent of the vote.[6] The elections of 1977 dealt a heavy blow to the party, which then secured only 11.6 per cent of the vote. Badly split even before the elections, members of the New Forces formed an independent grouping and others left EDIK (the name of the party since 1976) after the original leader, George Mavros, was replaced by John Zigdis. The New Democracy Party – with its opening towards the centre – attracted some wayward EDIK deputies – while others joined John Pesmazoglu's Social Democratic party (KODISO) which aspired to create a modern alternative to the expiring Centre Union. The elections of October 1981 eradicated centre parties from Parliament altogether, although Pesmazoglu won a seat in the European Parliament. The greatest percentage of former Centre Union votes went to PASOK, thus moderating its constituency.

### The Communist Party

The Greek Communist Party (KKE) was legalized in 1974, and it entered the elections of that year with a unified list of candidates, though its ranks had split into a segment loyal to Moscow (known as the 'Exterior' by its opponents) and one of Eurocommunist orientation, called the Greek Communist Party of the Interior. In the 1977 elections the 'Exterior', which inherited the bulk of the party membership, voters and newspaper circulation, outnumbered the 'Interior' five-to-one. It won 9.3 per cent of the vote while the 'Interior' – part of a coalition with four socialist and progressive groupings – shared only a 2.7 per cent with its partners. The foreign policy of the 'Exterior' is almost totally in line with that of the Soviet Union and is therefore opposed to the EEC and, of course, to NATO. The 'Interior' abandoned the concept of the 'dictatorship of the proletariat', adopted democratic pluralism and favoured Greek entry into the EEC. An influential spokesman for the 'Interior', Leonidas Kyrkos, evaluated the Cyprus issue from the angle of American interests in the Middle East and considered that a war between Greece and Turkey would increase the dependence of both on the United States, as had been the case with Israel and Egypt after 1973. In the elections of October 1981 the 'Interior' failed to elect a deputy to Parliament, but Kyrkos won a place in the European Parliament. The 'Exterior' added 2 per cent to its previous performance and became the third party in a Parliament now of three parties. Given the adverse economic prospects and PASOK's inability to make all its promises true, the KKE may play a more active role in the coming years.

**The Role of the Armed Forces**
Greek security is naturally in part defined by the state of the armed forces, in terms not only of physical readiness but – perhaps more important – of the willingness of officers to restrain themselves from playing politics and to confine their activities to the protection of the homeland. The seven years of military dictatorship caused serious damage to the capabilities of the Greek forces. The mobilization of the Summer of 1974 revealed the degree of deterioration of discipline and morale as well as of equipment. Five years after the fall of the Junta, the Greek Army now appears to be free of the problems associated with its recent history. In terms of leadership, unity and equipment, it has probably never been in a better position to defend the homeland. Yet the obvious question in everyone's mind is whether civilian supremacy over the military has been firmly established, or whether a future political crisis will set the tanks rolling once again. A look at the background of post-war developments in the Greek officer corps may help to answer the question.

*The Post-War Period*
The officers of the post-war period possessed none of the ideological pluralism that their colleagues had shown in the inter-war years. The abortive coups of 1935, 1943 and 1944 had resulted in a clean sweep of anti-monarchical and left-wing officers, and the victory of the nationalist forces during the civil war determined the orientation of the post-war Army. The military after 1945 professed anti-Communism and exclusive allegiance to the King and, unlike officers of the past, they showed considerable social and educational homogeneity. Moreover, they were under the continuous influence of American military missions after 1946, due to their contribution during the Civil War. Although constitutionally under civilian control, the military soon found ample opportunity to develop independence from Government as a result of the autonomy permitted them. Military intrigue was often mistaken for patriotic zeal, and officers who strayed were merely admonished by the Government with fatherly understanding.

The official status of the Armed Forces was defined by a series of 'compulsory enactments' issued by the Sophoulis Government in December 1945. The Supreme Council of National Defence (ASEA), which included the three War Ministers, the Chiefs of the three branches of the Armed Forces and the Chiefs of the British Missions (without a vote), was chaired by the Prime Minister. ASEA dealt with the general orientation of defence, the appointment of the military high command and the allocation of military expenditures – thus confirming the supremacy of the civilians over the military.[7]

However, 'the institutional affirmation' of the tendency towards the autonomy of the military occurred in January 1949, with the appointment of General Papagos as Commander-in-Chief of the Armed Forces. ASEA was replaced by a War Council with purely decorative functions, while the Commander-in-Chief acquired complete authority over all military matters.[8]

His suggestions, which could even include the imposition of martial law, were binding for the Minister of Defence. Papagos' extraordinary powers, which were given to him due to the emergency conditions caused by the Civil War, concentrated authority over military decisions and facilitated the establishment of American influence, unhindered by political opposition.

Although the post of Commander-in-Chief was abolished after Papagos' resignation in 1951, a precedent of institutionalized military autonomy had been set up and a group of officers had found a new patron in the person of the honoured Commander-in-Chief.

The Civil War ended in September 1949 but it became a point of reference which continued to live on, and it had brought into being a segment of the military with an excuse to covet its aspects of autonomy throughout the 1950s and 1960s. This was not an army of state-builders or modernizers but rather the trump card of the state against the 'internal enemy'.[9]

The most active post-war clandestine association of officers was founded in the Middle East in 1943 and assumed the initials IDEA (most probably in 1945) which stood for 'Holy Bond of Greek Officers'.[10] The foremost objective of the organization was to purge the armed forces of elements that failed to conform to its own high standards of nationalist purity, so that the military would serve 'the nation rather than political parties'.[11] Despite the sonorous language of its charter, the organization gradually became a pole of attraction not for the military establishment, which enjoyed royal favour, but for a less distinguished group of somewhat disgruntled officers. Papagos, a national symbol by 1950 and a threat to the royal monopoly of influence in the Armed Forces, became, perhaps unknowingly, the natural leader for this breed of right-wingers who felt that their advancement was blocked by a political and military establishment with intolerably liberal and leftist sympathies.[12]

The abortive coup of 31 May 1951 was launched by the IDEA conspirators in order to forestall Papagos' resignation from the army, which had been brought about by his clash with the monarchy. The failure of this coup and the punishment of its protagonists were more apparent than real. As matters turned out, its objectives were better served by its failure. Papagos, whose timely intervention stopped the half-baked conspiracy in its tracks, emerged as the only figure who could exert influence on all levels of the military structure. Once he became a popularly elected Prime Minister, he not only reinstated most of the dismissed members of IDEA but he also tolerated the foundation of a parallel military establishment, rival to the Throne, which would in the future threaten the very regime it was supposed to be guarding. Papagos merely averted a schism which reappeared sixteen years later. By postponing it, he in fact made it more dangerous.

*Intervention in Politics*

The reasons that brought about the 1967 military intervention were varied. Detente reduced the importance of the army as guarantor of internal order. The furious efforts of the military regime in 1967 to rekindle the 'red peril' were not only an exercise in self-deception and rationalization but also the last attempt of the Junta to preserve unity among military networks that had ceased to be of the same mind.

The second important reason for intervention was the conflict between the Throne and Parliament which flared during the Papandreou years. The main cause of the dispute was the control of the armed forces, but it resulted in the emancipation of certain military networks from both political and as royal tutelage. It was these networks, with a marked contempt for politicians as well as for the Court, that sought to save Greece from 'chaos'.

The least discussed cause of the 1967 coup, but a vital one nonetheless, was the professional grievances of a certain segment of the officer corps. The sudden expansion of the army during the Civil War and reduced opportunities for promotion afterwards caused congestion in the middle ranks. The traditional pyramid of promotions (whereby one third of the officer corps advances in rank, one third remains stationary and the last third is retired) was further undermined by political and royal favouritism, so that most officers were retired in the rank of Brigadier. This practice undermined the advancement of able officers and preserved the least qualified (who would otherwise have been retired). It was officers of the latter type who became willing clients of the 1967 regime.

The anomaly of 1967 created vacancies in the army which were filled not on merit but rather according to loyalty to the regime. Although favouritism had never been absent from promotion, the insecure dictatorship surpassed all precedent in its exercise of nepotism. Some 3,000 officers were retired or dismissed between 1967 and 1972, and they were replaced by friends of the Junta.[13] Since military men involved in politics rarely have time to improve their professional skills, the promotions of 1967–72 seriously undermined the competence of the army. Furthermore, congestion of the middle ranks reached an absurd level. In 1974 officers between the ranks of Lieutenant and Captain formed 43 per cent of the entire officer corps, while those in the ranks of Major and Colonel amounted to no less than 54 per cent.[14]

The institutional structure of the armed forces was also significantly transformed by the Junta. Before the conspirators firmly established themselves in power, the Armed Forces were governed by Law 2387 of 1953, according to which each Chief of Staff (Army, Navy and Air Force) was separately responsible for his own service to the Minister of Defence who was vested with the highest authority over military matters. The General Staff of National Defence co-ordinated the activities of the three services without in fact having any authority over them.[15]

Papadopoulos created the position of the Chief of the Armed Forces, thus depriving the Minister of Defence of his authority and the Chiefs of Staff of any autonomy within their separate branches. By concentrating power, the dictator was in a better position to control it. This concentration of military authority, which, among the other NATO members, exists only in Turkey, ultimately contributed to the decline in morale and initiative of the separate Service Staffs.[16] Their performance during the Cyprus crisis of 1974 leaves little doubt about the failure of the system. The institution of the General Staff, however, was highly praised by American military experts, despite the fact that such an institution is prohibited in the United States by the National Security Act of 1947.[17]

*After the Junta*
The Act of August 1977 determining the present structure of command in the Armed Forces did away with the innovations of the Junta. According to Act 660, the Government alone is responsible for national defence. The Supreme Council of National Defence (ASEA) is made up of the Prime Minister, the Deputy Prime Minister, the Ministers of Defence, Co-ordination, Foreign Affairs, Public Order and the Chief of the General Staff. Besides drafting defence policy, it appoints the Chief of the General Staff and the Chiefs of Staff and it makes most other important military appointments.[18] The decisions of ASEA are based on the recommendations of the Defence Minister who is in turn advised by the Chief of the General Staff. Since the Minister has no direct experience of the problems in the Armed Forces, his decisions are obviously influenced by his military advisers, that is by the Chiefs of Staff.[19] This state of affairs is seen by some as creating separate areas of autonomy for the military which may prove dangerous for future parliamentary regimes.[20] Others, who fought for the dissolution of the Junta's military institutions, have argued that areas of autonomy for the branches of the Armed Forces will guarantee the development of a more professional mentality among officers and will act as a deterrent against joint conspiracies.[21]

Be that as it may, institutional measures are rarely of value if they are not accompanied by the officers' personal concern for the advancement of their professional competence and backed by a civilian culture which frowns upon the politicization of the army. Preventing partisan views from entering the Armed Forces, however, is one thing; isolating the forces from any public scrutiny is quite another. According to Article 68, Paragraph 2, of the 1975 Constitution, Parliament can form Committees of Enquiry after a two-fifths vote in the Assembly on all matters except those of a military nature – which require an absolute majority.[22] Withholding information and creating a *cordon sanitaire* around the Armed Forces can be as counterproductive as the tendency to absolve the officers from all responsibility during the seven years of military dictatorship. During the electoral campaign of 1977 only N. Konstantopoulos of the 'Alliance' (a coalition of left-wing groupings) spoke his mind about the Greek Military. Other parties, including PASOK, bypassed the issue or simply attributed the entire responsibility for the military dictatorship to politicians who had allegedly undermined discipline in the Army before the Junta seized power.

There is at present a consensus in Parliament on military issues. With the exception of occasional references to an incomplete purge of Junta elements, the officer corps is rarely criticized. The seizure of power by the Junta is attributed in somewhat simplistic terms to a 'conspiracy of a few fools' (*afrones*), and the former Minister of Defence often reassured Parliament that civilian supremacy had been firmly established. Questions regarding the military budget are usually settled by general agreement, and the opposition does not now press for military cuts.

Although little information is available concerning the present state of mind in the Armed Forces, there is no indication that the Greek officers corps is not happily occupied with the exclusive task of protecting the homeland from external threats.

There is no way of predicting future developments, but there are ways of preventing the future from evolving in the wrong direction. An effective democratic education at the Military Academy, coupled with skills allowing middle-ranking officers to face retirement without alarm, could certainly work to minimize conspiratorial thoughts. Other prescriptions for a lasting 'cure' of the Greek military could include autonomy within their own sphere of professional expertise, freedom from political pressures and the abolition of activities outside their main line of interest.

Internal and external security considerations are intertwined. The events of the Summer of 1974 give ample proof of the outcome when the internal and the external fronts are challenged simultaneously.

**Economic Aspects of Greek Security**
It has been said that Greece fits the description neither of an under-developed nor of a peripheral economy. Between 1962 and 1978 an average growth rate of 6.6 per cent per year was achieved despite economic turbulence. Productivity grew by 7.3 per cent per year and *per capita* income reached $US 3,000. During the same period industrial production rose by 9 per cent per year, industrial employment by 3.3 per cent (agricultural labour constitutes only about 20 per cent of the total labour force) and agricultural production by 4.2 per cent. Unemployment declined to the lowest level in Europe and the return of guest workers from Germany did not alter the picture.

Industrial production forms 60 per cent of Greece's total exports in value, one third of which goes to the Middle East and North Africa.[23] Diversification of trade precludes dependence on a single market, while production has generally overtaken demand. Dependence on external energy sources has somewhat diminished. In 1978 foreign capital inflows constituted only 20 per cent of the $US 3 billion invested in the Greek economy. Some Greek economists suggest that in strictly financial terms Greece therefore is now very much less dependent on foreign capital. Such dependence as remains, they claim, is due to political constraints of the past rather than to the nature of the Greek economy. Finally, the size of the Greek-owned merchant fleet is yet another factor which may contribute to greater economic independence.[24]

Other evaluations, however, point to contrary conclusions. Economic growth is seen as import-based, constantly inflating the foreign trade deficit. This deficit is covered by immigrant and merchant marine remittances, tourism and foreign loans.[25] Should one or more of these sources of foreign exchange decline and inflation continue to grow, the positive picture of the economy may well be reversed. The emigration of labourers in the 1960s is seen as a mixed blessing. A potentially cheap input in production (labour) was unwisely replaced by the importation of expensive foreign capital. Industrial growth was therefore to a large extent based on foreign capital and knowledge, especially in those sectors concerned with higher levels of technology. Domestic investment has been concentrated more in light industries and in the less productive sectors such as construction.[26]

Moreover, there has been a negative trend in Greek economic affairs since 1979. The data for 1980 presented by the Governor of the Bank of Greece pointed out that inflation (running at 26 per cent) and stagnant production were the chief economic problems facing the Government (and this is still the case). Gross domestic product at constant prices in 1980 rose by only 1.9 per cent compared with 3.7 per cent in 1979. Gross investment also dropped in that year due to reduced activity in the construction sector and to reductions in public expenditure. Despite the slowing down of economic activity, the rate of urban unemployment remains low, and the official estimate of the rate of unemployment in 1980 was 2.5 per cent compared with 2.2 per cent in 1979. Present domestic and international economic conditions would appear to rule out the possibility of overcoming the recession by the adoption of expansionist policies. Predictably the New Democracy Government pursued a restrictive set of economic policies, but efforts to restrain the growth of money supply met with only partial success. By the end of 1980 the balance of payments deficit was $US 2,217 million, compared with $US 1,882 million the previous year. The oil import bill alone increased by $US 947 million over the same period. High interest rates continued into 1981 as well as efforts to restrain the growth of money supply, but it did not appear that monetary measures alone could cope with the economic situation.

Shortly before the elections, Papandreou told an American journalist: 'They [the New Democracy technocrats] believe Greece is a capitalist country, but it is really on the periphery of capitalism, and has many pre-capitalist characteristics, our huge underground economy being one example. This means that huge doses of Government intervention and planning will be needed to bring Greece up to par with the developed capitalist nations'.[27]

The state has played a paramount, if not always efficient, role in Greek economic development. Besides contributing its own resources, it has provided the infrastructure and the legislative pre-conditions to encourage the private sector. It was also responsible for negotiating the major foreign investment deals which were often heavily criticized. PASOK's moderate doses of state intervention, however, are producing little result in curbing inflation, improving the balance of payments or increasing national productivity. At the end of 1982 Papandreou is still faced with most of the economic problems he inherited from the previous Administration. In spite of an extensive change of guard in public positions and a reshuffling of the civil service, PASOK has yet to produce a visible alternative to the familiar recipes of anti-inflationary and austerity measures. With public consumption further restricted by the impact of such measures, and a fall in private investment for the third consecutive year, Papandreou realized that much of what he had hoped to achieve would have to be deferred. The July 1982 Cabinet reshuffle indicated that the foreign-based technocrats of the party carried the day. Gerassimos Arsenis, a former director of UNCTAD who was PASOK's Governor of the Bank of Greece, became the Minister of National Economy (a newly created post), and it may be predicted that he will attempt to reduce the budget deficit inherited by the previous Administration and to ensure implementation of austere budgetary and monetary policies. Although 'socialization' of key industries amounted to establishing supervisory committees with representatives of employees, management and local government, the ultimate role of the state in the economy is still to be resolved.[28]

Membership of the EEC was seen by Karamanlis as a kind of insurance against such internal anomalies as the coup of 1967 and perhaps Turkish demands on Greek sovereignty. Whether this appraisal is correct remains to be seen, but the economic implications of being a member of the Community have become the object of much discussion in Greece. Somewhere between the enthusiastic supporters and the emotional opposition are those who see it as the least evil of the possible alternatives. Membership may provide security for certain spheres of economic activity (agriculture in particular) but at the price of possible damage to others (such as industry). To some, Europe appears to offer a genuine alternative to submission to exclusive US influence, and these would even predict a future economic conflict between the US and the EEC.[29] To others, Europe is as dependent on the US for defence as Greece, and so the EEC does not offer genuine emancipation from the influence of the US.

At present the European Economic Community possesses no instrument of crisis management, and, with the exception of Ireland, its members rely on NATO for their own security. The leading economic power in the EEC, West Germany, has attached great importance to the efficient functioning of the Alliance and has often given the matter priority over other considerations. While aiming at a renegotiation of the original agreement of accession, Papandreou has retreated from his original promise to submit the future of Greece's membership of the Community to a plebiscite.

## IV. THE NATURE OF GREEK SECURITY IN THE 1980s

**The Link with the West and Turkey**

On 18 October 1980, George Rallis' Government announced its decision to bring the country back into NATO's military arm. The Alliance had previously overcome Turkey's insistence that Greek reintegration should be preceded by a reconsideration of operational responsibilities in the Aegean. The decision was received with relief by NATO members, but it generated mixed feelings in Greece. Criticism of the Atlantic Alliance, which was once confined to the left of the Greek political spectrum, became widespread during the Junta period, and especially after the Turkish invasion of Cyprus in the Summer of 1974. Voices of caution pointing to the practical advantages of membership were drowned by the moral tone of the opposition. The chief objection to re-entry was one of principle, namely that the reason for withdrawal – the military occupation of 40 per cent of Cyprus by Turkey – had not been resolved.

On a more practical level, Turkey's decision of 22 February 1980 to withdraw her six-year-old claim to air-traffic-control rights in the eastern half of the Aegean marked an improvement of relations which continued until April 1981. At the beginning of March 1981, the Greek Foreign Minister, K. Mitsotakis, announced a series of modifications to the air-traffic arrangements within the Athens FIR designed to facilitate the movement of Turkish aircraft in the Aegean airspace. These included a reduction by approximately one half of the extent of the Terminal Control Area of the airport on the island of Lemnos and various adjustments to the upper and lower altitude limits of several Aegean air corridors.[1] These unilateral measures made in good faith were criticized by the opposition in the Greek Parliament but were welcomed by the Turkish Foreign Ministry as 'gestures of good will'.[2] However, while Graeco–Turkish discussions over questions of the Aegean air-space were taking place, Greek sovereign air-space was repeatedly violated by Turkish aircraft during April 1981.[3]

Violations of Greek air-space and territorial waters also occurred in May, and these were interpreted as Turkey's way of registering her opposition to the ten-mile limit of Greek air-space and served to remind her allies that the question of operational responsibilities was still unresolved. The latter issue has acquired a certain urgency in view of the impending assumption of operational responsibilities by the Larissa NATO headquarters. NATO authorities urge Greece to consider the question of responsibilities *after* the Headquarters become operational, but Turkey will not even agree to an interim arrangement whereby the pre-1974 *status quo* would remain in force, let alone to recognize a permanent state of affairs along those lines.[4] Since Greece considers this an issue of cardinal importance to her security, there is no apparent way out of the impasse.

Although Greece has often complained that the United States and West Germany have been partial towards Turkey, it is ultimately Greece's own traditional compliance in the face of Western pressure that accounts particularly for her disadvantageous bargaining position within the Alliance. The reasons for this compliance are to be found in the foundations of the modern Greek state as well as in its subsequent development and dependence upon foreign powers. During World War II Greece joined the Allied cause (without even being granted a treaty of alliance) and suffered occupation and civil war. The fact that a great power became instrumental in resolving her internal problems determined Greece's post-war diplomacy as well as her defence policy.

The entire post-war orientation of Greek defence was based on the American belief that Greece's main security concern was of an internal rather than an external nature. According to a National Security Report of 1949, Greece was to have 'a military establishment capable of maintaining internal security in order to avoid Communist domination, while Turkey was designated with a military establishment of sufficient size and effectiveness to insure her continued resistance to Soviet pressures.' The Greek army was therefore primarily supplied and organized to face the internal Communist threat. A modification of the original report, appearing two years later, included an external operational assignment for the Greek forces, but it made clear that Greece would not be supplied with the necessary materiel to repel a foreign attack and, furthermore, that the United States could make no commitment to come to the aid of her ally if the latter were faced with an external attack. Greece was nevertheless expected 'through certain limited accessories to cause some delay to Soviet and satellite forces in case of global war.'[5]

Given the allocation of defence roles between Greece and Turkey, it is not difficult to assess the implications of their joint entrance into NATO for the former's security. Whereas Greece was primarily geared to face an internal threat and ill-equipped to resist a Soviet attack, she was nevertheless expected to aid Turkey, which was presumably the primary target in the Balkans, and so ran the risk of attracting enemy reprisals.

Of course Greece is no longer divided by civil strife, her economy has made important strides since the 1950s, and her defensive position was transformed after 1974. She continues, however, to lag behind Turkey in US estimation of her comparative strategic importance (for reasons which are obvious).

On the other hand, since Atatürk, Turkish diplomacy has pursued a successful course of non-involvement in international conflicts. Although Turkey signed a Treaty of Affiliation with Britain and France in October 1939, she kept out of World War II and, with the exception of the Cold-war period, retained her relative independence in international politics. With the emergence of detente and the relaxation of tensions between the super-powers, some of the urgency which governed relations between Turkey and the United States disappeared. Refusing to forfeit the tangible benefits deriving from her value to the Western Alliance, Turkey resumed her traditional independent posture, constantly reminding her allies that she could either seek solutions to her problems elsewhere or, more simply, that she could still prove a significant liability if she refused to play her part as host to American bases. The loss of Iran and her own internal misfortunes have enhanced Turkey's importance for the United States.

Since 'loss' of Greece has never entered into American calculations, it is ultimately the thought of Turkey neutral or on the enemy side which haunts the American military establishment. It is not without some justification that Greece fears that she will be asked to pay the price of an effort to reinforce Turkey's faith in the Western Alliance. It is therefore to Greece's advantage to seek maximum autonomy within the NATO framework.

In spite of differences on the security level, there is considerable Greek admiration for Turkey's ability to maintain an autonomous stance in her relationships with the West and the Great Powers. Flexible diplomacy and Turkish patriotism have won the country sixty years of uninterrupted peace and, except for the Cold-war period, a prudent relationship with both the super-powers. Turkey's Western commitment in the 1950s should not be attributed to American penetration but rather to the goals set and the decisions taken by Turkish policy-makers based on wide domestic support. Furthermore, no national division on the scale of the Greek Civil War has so far encouraged foreign powers to intervene directly in Turkey's internal affairs.

Some Greek politicians also tend to compare Greece's rather ineffectual withdrawal from NATO in 1974 with Turkey's reaction to the American embargo. Instead of leaving NATO in high dudgeon, the Turks at the end of July 1975 suspended the operation of all but one of their American bases and then successfully renegotiated their defence agreements and ensured the lifting of the arms embargo.

European Community membership may well benefit Greece on certain fronts, but it will probably disappoint those Greeks who believe that it will also constitute a guarantee against future Turkish aggression. As noted earlier, the EEC possesses no instrument of crisis management and, excepting Ireland, its members belong also to NATO. West Germany, moreover, considers Turkey vital for the defence of NATO's south-eastern flank. In 1978 Germany exerted considerable pressure on the United States to lift the arms embargo imposed on Turkey after the 1974 invasion of Cyprus, although she has also been in the vanguard of those urging a return to democratic rule in Turkey. Furthermore, Western Europeans have already taken measures to avoid the Graeco–Turkish dispute spilling over into the EEC and to mitigate the political effects of Greece's accession on their own relations with Turkey.[6]

Membership of the EEC and NATO will also entail fashioning Greece's relations with the United States with reference to that larger context.[7] Greece may support European efforts at preserving detente and arms control by offering her services in the Balkan region, where she now enjoys good relations with her Communist neighbours.

European attitudes towards the US, however, have changed in two important respects during the past seven years: confidence in American leadership has been shaken; and America's economic problems have had political implications in her relations with her allies. Europeans now believe that they are entitled to 'more attention, consideration and consultation than in the arrogant days of unlimited and undisputed American world power'.[8] Greece also shares those European attitudes vis-à-vis the Eastern Bloc which have caused American discomfort.[9] Most European countries have neutralist and Communist sections of public opinion to placate, and they have tried to take advantage of detente and to avoid involvement in wider super-power disputes.

It is in this wider context that the electoral outcome of 18 October 1981 in Greece must also be assessed. Besides the residual tensions in US–Greek relations arising from American support for the Junta and for the Turks over the subsequent Graeco–Turkish problems, European and American security perceptions no longer appear to be wholly compatible. Economic recession, which drives both Western and Eastern Europeans into closer co-operation, and the controversy over the need to deploy new nuclear weapons to counter Soviet superiority, have not left Greek politics unaffected. The non-aligned tendencies of the Papandreou Government, which would have been unthinkable in the past, do not provoke serious criticism from the Greek opposition. Notwithstanding Papandreou's current suggestion that the terms of Greece's entrance into the EEC should be revised, it is likely that his Government will in fact tend to align itself with a European policy that seeks a more autonomous relationship with the East.

Developments in the Aegean and Cyprus will largely determine the future of Greece's relations with NATO and the United States. Given the division of PASOK into moderate and radical wings, moderation on the foreign policy front may be essential to offset the radicalizing effect of a declining economy on politics. Thus if the United States and Turkey prove less understanding of Greece's position, the anti-American tendencies within PASOK will prevail, encouraged by the traditional nationalism of the liberal right. External pressures promote consensus at home, and only a relaxation of tension would allow the opposition to resume an effective stance towards the foreign policy of the Government.

## The Soviet and Communist Threat

For the past fifteen years the Soviet Union has taken care to avoid provocative gestures that might encourage dissension between Greece and Turkey. Predictably, she has followed an opportunistic policy in the dispute between the two NATO allies. Although championing Cypriot integrity throughout the 1960s, the Soviet Union not only remained passive during the 1974 invasion but also invited Turkish Foreign Minister Erkin to Moscow at the end of October 1974. A year later, at the opening ceremony of the Soviet-financed steel mill at Iskenderun, the two countries agreed to 'draw up a political document on friendly relations and co-operation'.[10] Furthermore, during the NATO Summit of May 1977 in Washington, Turkish Prime Minister Ecevit declared that his country felt no threat from the USSR and should therefore reconsider her obsolete defence policy.[11] A year later, while the fate of the arms embargo on Turkey was being discussed in Congress, Ecevit visited Moscow and an agreement between the two states was signed and entitled 'The Principles of Good Neighbourly and Friendly Relations.'[12] Today Turkey ranks as the largest recipient of Soviet aid among the developing countries.

Spurred on by the Soviet–Turkish *rapprochement* and by her problems with NATO, Greece has sought a way out of her impasse with the Soviet Union (which lasted for 50 years). Contacts were initially established in such fields as industry, shipping, commerce, tourism and sport. In January 1977 a long-term trade accord was concluded, and two years later Greece secured the supply of 1.2 million tons of Soviet oil. The visit of Foreign Minister Rallis to Moscow in 1978 was followed by the establishment of Consulates in Thessaloniki and Odessa, intended to facilitate mercantile marine co-operation between the two countries. This Graeco-Soviet thaw was highlighted by two events, both of which caused considerable speculation in the West during the Autumn of 1979. Three weeks before Mr Karamanlis visited Moscow in October 1979, an agreement was concluded between a private Greek company and the Soviet Union which offered the latter shipyard repair facilities in the Neorion docks on the Aegean island of Syros. Although it was explicitly stated that armed ships were excluded from the deal, the agreement raised protests from the US State Department which, in turn, provoked bitter statements from even the pro-Western Greek press to the effect that Greece was free to conduct her own trade policy and resented foreign interference.[13] In 1981, presumably under pressure from the United States, the Greek Government obliged the firm to alter the terms of the agreement. While the yards remained opened for the repair of merchant ships, they were closed to auxiliary units of the Soviet Mediterranean Fleet.[14] After the accession of the PASOK Government, however, the firm was allowed to proceed with the original agreement. The Greek Government pointed out that the Soviet repair orders rejected by the Greek firm had been placed with French shipyards.

The state visit of Karamanlis to the Soviet Union of 1–5 October 1979, although not intended to explore possibilities of a fresh alignment with the Soviet Union, did produce a considerable relaxation of tensions between the two countries. Continued improvements in Graeco–Bulgarian relations have made the potential Soviet threat even more remote.

Whether their evaluation of Soviet intent is correct or not, the fact remains that both NATO allies of the Southern Flank consider the Warsaw Pact threat as one which is not of immediate concern. Turkey is currently preoccupied with her internal problems and with the resurgence of Kurdish nationalism, which has been reinforced by the breakdown of central authority in Iran and the subsequent war with Iraq. The Soviet Union has not tried to make political capital in Turkey either by encouraging left-wing activities or by condemning the military regime which took over in September 1980.[15]

Greece, on the other hand, is mainly preoccupied with what is perceived as a threat from Turkey. Greeks of all political shades are convinced that, although the Turkish regime is incapable of offensive action, due to its present economic and social problems, it has nevertheless staked its claims for future demands on Greek sovereign rights.[16]

Neither Athens nor Ankara believes that NATO considers the Eastern Mediterranean theatre to be as vital as that of Central Europe. It appears that most scenarios of conflict drafted by NATO and the US place more emphasis on the Central European Front and consider the Flanks of secondary importance.[17] Be that as it may, the somewhat relaxed attitude would be bound to change if a crisis in Yugoslavia brought a pro-Soviet leadership to power, or if Albania were to invite the Soviet Union to return the naval base at Vlöne which she was forced to abandon in 1961. A Soviet foothold on the Adriatic could make communications between the Southern Flank of NATO and its Central Command much more difficult. Equally, if Greece were lost to NATO, the movement of war materiel by sea to Turkey and Italy in wartime would be hopelessly disrupted.[18]

In the event of war between the two Blocs, Soviet *Backfire* bombers and SS-20 missiles (as well as the Soviet 5th Escadra) will prove serious threats to the American fleet in the Mediterranean. Greek and Turkish aircraft would be expected to intercept Soviet aircraft flying out of the Crimea, and therefore airfields in both countries would probably come under attack. With or without Turkish approval, the Americans will almost certainly mine the Dardanelles to prevent further deployment of Soviet vessels into the Aegean. Aircraft from Sixth Fleet carriers could deliver nuclear weapons on Southern Soviet bases as, in future, could ground-or sea-launched cruise missiles. With nuclear warheads stockpiled in Italy, Greece and Turkey, these countries may expect to suffer counter-strikes or even pre-emptive attack.

If Greece were incapacitated or neutralized, Turkey would be isolated from the nearest friendly land border by 700 miles of inaccessible terrain. Warsaw Pact thrusts from Bulgaria could then be directed against the Straits without fear of a flank attack. NADGE sites which provide warning of air attacks on Italy, Turkey or the Sixth Fleet would themselves be attacked, and sea communications between the Western and the Eastern Mediterranean would become a great deal more difficult.[19] If, on the other hand, Turkey was incapacitated or chose to remain neutral, Greece's eastern flank would be exposed to Soviet naval and air attacks and Warsaw Pact forces would attempt to reach the Aegean through the narrow strip of Western Thrace, again without fear of flank attack from the east. The Soviet forces already in the Mediterranean would, however, still be faced with a Greek archipelago in which naval, air and missile forces might be hard to silence.

In peacetime, Soviet interests in the Eastern Mediterranean are somewhat different. Turkey's agreeably loose interpretation of the Montreux Treaty allows a steady flow of Soviet vessels into the Aegean, from where Soviet ships must follow a careful course through the Greek archipelago in order to reach North Africa, the Middle East or the Atlantic.

From February 1982, the Soviet press (*Pravda, Izvestia* and *TASS*) inaugurated a new policy towards Greece which is not confined simply to bilateral issues. The Soviet Union addressed Graeco–Turkish issues in terms favourable to Greece. It is not without significance that this 'opening' has more or less coincided with the renewal of US–Greek discussion (in May 1982) on the future of American bases in Greece.

**Future Prospects and Security Options for Greece**

Whether or not PASOK fulfils its promises to pursue a policy of non-alignment to a much greater extent, it is clear that Greek policy towards the Western Alliance is entering a new phase. Although speculation about the degree of change is hardly consistent, there is little doubt that Greece will attempt to assert her independence from foreign influence considerably more than she has done.[20]

In a country where foreign policy issues tend to play a decisive role in the outcome of elections, the erosion of US and NATO credibility during the last thirteen years has paved the way for PASOK's rise, first to influence and now to power. The problems of the economy notwithstanding (and these have become more serious recently), it has been the marked commitment of the Reagan Administration to Turkey and the failure of the moderate tactics of the Karamanlis and Rallis Administrations to achieve a *rapprochement* with Turkey that have convinced even right-wing voters to support the more nationalistic and activist PASOK.

Although he condemns power blocs in principle, Andreas Papandreou will not fail to exploit the opportunities afforded him by operating within the Western Alliance, and he will make full use of the rights afforded Greece by her NATO membership in order to safeguard Greek security. For instance, Greece will want to ensure that Spain's entry into NATO will not alter the operational responsibilities in the Eastern Mediterranean in any way that might affect Greece's interests. She has bargained her compliance in the matter of Spanish entry for a formula that will protect all NATO countries from predator members (but with a particular, if undeclared, eye on Turkey). Germany and Italy appear to be interested in leading the search for such a formula.[21] It is precisely such practical concerns and pragmatic policies which may irritate PASOK's left wing. Papandreou may find it hard to contain the kind of nationalistic left-wing fervour that his campaign undoubtedly released as he moves carefully into dialogue and compromise with Turkey.

Although reintegration into the military structure of NATO was decided in October 1980, there is as yet no sign that an agreement will be reached concerning Turkey's demands for the reconsideration of operational responsibilities in the Aegean. Neither Greece nor Turkey seem likely to move from their positions on the matter, but it is ultimately the United States which will play the decisive role in concluding the conflict.

Some Greek analysts question the validity of the American view that Turkey offers comparative advantages as an ally over Greece; others, however, accept American appraisals at face value and point to the implicit danger of relying on a biased mediator and ally. NATO and the US clearly view the dispute between the Southern Flank states as a nuisance which must be solved in an equitable way. The future significance of the problem tends to be played down and, in somewhat simplistic terms, is attributed mainly to historical and emotional factors which were allegedly used by politicians and journalists to serve political ends. However, the fact that the issue has been extensively exploited by political parties underlines its importance for both countries. For Turkey, extended control over the Eastern half of the Aegean would enhance the strategic value of her territory. Her strategic location has already been more effective than any other factor or asset in securing foreign aid and loans. For Greece the alienation of her Eastern islands would amount to loss of sovereign territory and be a major blow to her economy.

Greek interpretations of Turkish motives abound. The least sophisticated emphasize the technique of 'distraction' allegedly employed by the Turkish Government to divert public discontent from internal social issues to external adventure. Others would point to rapid population increase and the declining economy as leading to a revival of Turkish expansionism. The third, and perhaps most convincing, interpretation focuses on Turkey's evolving relationship with the West and the United States. Developments in Iran have tended to increase Turkey's geostrategic importance in American eyes, not least because Turkish air bases could become of crucial significance for any attempt by US tactical aircraft to interdict any Soviet move to the Upper Persian Gulf. Greece fears that Turkey is trying to maximize her bargaining power to secure a firm foothold in the Aegean.

Regardless of interpretations, Greece is bound to pursue a number of objectives to ensure both the independence of her national security from external constraints and a continuous supply of military hardware. The latter objective is being pursued by improving the domestic arms industry and maintenance facilities. Recent developments include a rifle assembly plant (destined shortly to go into full production), ammunition factories, facilities to upgrade elderly tanks and the production of communication systems. The core of Greece's defence industry consists of the $300 million plant of the Hellenic Aerospace Industry located at Tanagra. It can overhaul, repair, modify and convert military and commercial aircraft, accessories, engines and electronics. It aspires to service commercial and military airfleets and to manufacture some air-frame spares. The Hellenic Shipyard near Piraeus has been building a series of ten fast patrol craft for the Navy and Coast Guard as well as six *La Combattante II* fast missile craft. There are reports that the shipyard is also laying the keel of a frigate for the Hellenic Navy. The Government-owned firm Steyr Hellas is expected to receive an order for $500 million worth of equipment including 3,500 heavy-duty military trucks and engines.[22]

In parallel with expansion of domestic procurement, Greece is also seeking to diversify her sources of military supply to avoid the foreign policy constraints imposed by reliance on a single provider. The current and prospective scale of Turkey's power may, however, require a more drastic solution. Given the Turkish rate of population growth and the increasing US military aid to Turkey,[23] Greek policy-makers cannot exclude the option of developing nuclear weapons. While still a member of the opposition, Papandreou mentioned the nuclear option (especially since rumours held that Turkey was co-operating with Pakistan to develop her own nuclear weapons) while simultaneously commiting himself to a nuclear-free zone in the Balkans.[24] Although the number and location of US and NATO nuclear weapons based in the Balkans is classified, it can be assumed that they are antiquated and incapable of striking targets deep in Soviet territory. As Platias and Rydell put it, 'When these modest capabilities are compared to the 7,000 [now 6,000] aggregate total of European theatre nuclear weapons it is apparent that the Greek and Turkish nuclear contribution to NATO is minimal. Furthermore, the modest Soviet deployment of short-range *Scud* and *FROG* missiles in Romania and Bulgaria could probably be removed without seriously jeopardising the required balance'.[25] Be that as it may, withdrawal will nevertheless mean further alienation with the West. Papandreou would have had to assess the implications of such a decision (in view of his overall moderation towards the West during the Spring of 1982), but his visit to Sofia and Belgrade and the unwillingness of the Yugoslavs to discuss the nuclear-free-zone issue, may very well have relieved him from his dilemma.[26]

If the world continues to move from detente to confrontation with a resurgence of Cold-war attitudes and policies, Greece will drift further away from NATO, and US influence will diminish. She will have no alternative but to adjust her defence posture in order to face what is seen as the challenge from across the Aegean. PASOK certainly embodies that position. If a nuclear confrontation between the super-powers seemed to be imminent Greece might opt for non-alignment, and so might Turkey, given her past history. Both countries would then forfeit American patronage and be forced to rely on alternative sources of armaments. Neither might in that case be able to assume preponderance. If, on the other hand, a return to cold-war politics encouraged local confrontations between the clients of each bloc while containing the nuclear confrontation, Greece might turn back to NATO for support. Whether non-alignment secures an exemption from global involvement or not, more Greeks may come to feel that the risk of being drawn into nuclear holocaust is too large a price to pay for the sake of any political or social system, no matter how desirable. Keeping out of the way of the dinosaurs could become a major policy trend of the 1980s. National security in such an instance will be separated from wider defence considerations.

Relations between the super-powers will to a large extent dictate Greece's security options in the 1980s. If they demand conformity in the name of their own defence priorities and deny any alternative modes of local security, Greece's loyalty to NATO is likely to become severely strained.[27] If, however, a margin is allowed for independent decision-making, that margin will be much affected by domestic factors. Autonomy and flexibility in the realm of foreign policy presuppose the will of the state to run its own affairs and its readiness to grasp opportunities whenever they appear on the international scene.

# NOTES

## Introduction
[1] E. Kofos, *Greece and the Eastern Crisis, 1875–1878* (Thessaloniki: Institute of Balkan Studies, 1975), pp. 185–256; and D. Dakin, *The Greek Struggle in Macedonia 1897–1913* (Thessaloniki: Institute of Balkan Studies, 1966), pp. 360–74.
[2] J. Koliopoulos, *Greece and the British Connection, 1935–41* (Oxford: OUP, 1977), pp. 263–93.
[3] C. M. Woodhouse, *The Story of Modern Greece* (London OUP, 1968), p. 239.
[4] In response to Soviet accusations that Greece was violating Article 14, Paragraph 2, of the 1947 Treaty concerning the demilitarization of the Dodecanese, a top secret telegram was sent from the American Secretary of State to the Embassy in Athens on 29 July 1948, encouraging disregard of Communist pressure:

> Dept's opinion is that victorious ally who has been awarded territory as result Allied victory should not be placed in less favourable position than defeated enemy. Military clauses Italian Treaty after specifying destruction of fortifications and prohibitions for new constructions, state in several places that 'this prohibition does not include other types non-permanent fortifications and installations designed meet only requirements of internal character and local defence of frontiers' (Articles 47b, 48b, 50 para 4, Italian Treaty). Dept feels therefore that Greece has equal right to use Dodecanese military installations to maintain internal order or defend frontiers. (Marshall)

*US Foreign Relations Documents 1948*, Volume IV, pp. 116–17.
[5] J. Campbell and P. Sherrard, *Modern Greece* (London: Ernest Benn, 1968), p. 185.

## Chapter I
[1] H. E. Shear, 'Southern Flank of NATO' in *NATO's Fifteen Nations*, December–January 1979, Vol. 23, No. 6, pp. 7–8.
[2] *Ibid.*; see also Jesse W. Lewis, Jr., *The Strategic Balance in the Mediterranean* (Washington DC: American Enterprise Institute, 1976), pp. 10–11.
[3] *Ibid.*, pp. 2, 33–4.
[4] Foreign Affairs and National Defence Division, Congressional Research Service, Library of Congress, *United States Military Installations and Objectives in the Mediterranean* (Report), 27 March 1977 (Washington DC), pp. 30–32.
[5] *Ibid.*, pp. 32–5; also Lewis, *op. cit.* in note 2, pp. 23–4.
[6] M. Cremasco, 'NATO's Southern Flank in the East–West Balance', *Lo Spettatore Internazionale*, January–March 1979, pp. 13–23.
[7] N. Canakakis, *Greece and Turkey: Disputes over the Aegean Sea* unpublished paper, 1979, p. 93.
[8] European Security Working Group of Harvard Center for Science and International Affairs, 'Instability and Change on NATO's Southern Flank', *International Security*, Winter 1978, p. 151.
[9] James Brown, 'Challenges and Uncertainty, NATO's Southern Flank', *Air University Review*, May–June 1980, p. 4.
[10] For a full discussion of these issues, see Andrew Wilson, *The Aegean Dispute*, Adelphi Paper No. 155 (London: IISS, 1980).

## Chapter II
[1] According to the Greek census of 1928 there were 82,000 Bulgarians (Slavophones) in Greek Macedonia and practically none in Western Thrace. See Lada, *The Exchange of Minorities in Bulgaria, Greece and Turkey* (New York: Macmillan, 1932), pp. 27–8.
[2] John Kordatos, an articulate Communist opponent of the policy, accused the KKE's leadership in 1927 of having aligned itself with 'Bulgarian Chauvinism' (*Rizospastis*, 25 February, 1927) and resigned from the Party.
[3] E. Kofos, *Nationalism and Communism in Macedonia*, (Thessaloniki: Institute for Balkan Studies, 1964), pp. 121–2.
[4] *Ibid.* p. 188; see also R. P. King and S. E. Palmer, *Yugoslav Communism and the Macedonian Question* (Connecticut: Archon Press, 1971).
[5] Kofos, *op. cit.* in note 3, pp. 174–95.
[6] N. Zachariades, *Ten Years of Struggle* (in Greek), publisher unknown, 1951, p. 126.
[7] S. G. Xydis, 'Coups and Countercoups in Greece 1967–73', *Political Science Quarterly*, Vol. 89, No. 3, Fall 1974, pp. 534–5.
[8] N. Stavrou, 'Greek–American Relations and their Impact on Balkan Co-operation', in T. Couloumbis and John Iatrides (eds), *Greek–American Relations* (New York: Pella Publishing Co., 1980), p. 158.
[9] *Frankfurter Allgemeine*, 31 May 1977, correspondence by V. Meier; *To Vima* (Greek daily), articles by M. Ploumides, 7 and 30 July and 8 October 1978.
[10] *Christian Science Monitor*, 20 June 1978, correspondence by Eric Bourne; *To Vima*, article by M. Ploumides, 28 March 1978.
[11] *Avgi* (Greek Daily), editorial by S. Chrysostimides, 23 January 1977. Concerning the April 1979 meeting between Karamanlis and Zhivkov, see Romanian optimistic coverage in *Lumea*, 11–17 May 1979, p.16. Also, P. Mladenov, 'Bulgaria's Foreign Policy Today' in *International Affairs* (Moscow), No. 1, 1979, pp. 8–15.
[12] S. Valdin, 'The Significance and Structural Problems of Greece's Commercial Relations with Countries of State-Controlled Commerce' (in Greek), *Synchrona Themata*, Vol. 14, March 1982, p. 33
[13] *To Vima*, M. Ploumides, 9 July 1978; *Eleftherotypia* (Greek daily), correspondence by S. Oeconomou, 30 June 1978.
[14] Stavrou, *op. cit.* in note 8, p. 167.
[15] Karamanlis voiced his fears over the possible repercussions of the Sino–Soviet conflict in the Balkans in his 16 January 1979 speech at the Greek Parliament. *To Vima*, 17 and 18 March (articles by Linardatos and Ploumides) and 28 March 1979 (article by Efstathiades on Tito and Karamanlis).
[16] For an appraisal of a recent resurgence of the Macedonian issue, coinciding with Papandreou's visit in May to Belgrade, see K. Iordanides, 'Yugoslavia Poses the Macedonian Issue to Greece', *Kathimerini*, 28 May 1982.
[17] J. A. S. Grenville, *The Major International Treaties*

*1914–1973* (London: Methuen, 1974), p. 197.

[18] Bernard Lewis, *The Emergence of Modern Turkey* (London: OUP, 1968), pp. 297–302.

[19] The bibliography on the Cyprus issue is immense. For the best comprehensive account of the problem, see P. Kitromilides and T. Couloumbis, 'Ethnic Conflict in a Strategic Area: The Case of Cyprus' in the *Greek Review of Social Research*, No. 24 (Athens, 1975), pp. 271–91.

[20] The complicity of the Turkish Government was established by the 1960–61 trials of the Menderes Government. See Walter Weiker, *The Turkish Revolution 1960–61* (Washington DC: Brookings Institution, 1963), pp. 25–47. A number of prominent members of the Greek community were deported, and the unfavourable climate after 1955 precipitated a rapid exodus of ethnic Greeks from Istanbul. The community of 80,000 in 1950 has shrunk to 8,000, yet those who have to take up residence abroad remain Turkish citizens. Most of the Greek nationals (some 10,000) were expelled from Turkey in 1965 following a unilateral denunciation of the Agreement of Establishment Commerce and Navigation which had been part of the Venizelos–Ataturk Pact of 1930.

[21] Grivas died in January 1974.

[22] T. Ehrlich, *Cyprus 1958–1967* (Oxford: OUP, 1974), pp. 65–86.

[23] Quoted in L. Stern, *The Wrong Horse* (New York: Times Books, 1977), p. 117.

[24] On 6 July Makarios made public his accusation that Greek officers of the National Guard were linked with EOKA-B and demanded their removal from the island. The Junta answered on 15 July with the coup by the National Guard.

[25] Stern, *op. cit.* in note 23, p. 121.

[26] Nancy Crawshaw, *The Cyprus Revolt* (London: Allen and Unwin, 1978), p. 394.

[27] The chronology of intercommunal discussions was taken from Wilson (*op. cit.* in Ch. 1, note 10), pp. 31–5.

[28] For a comprehensive view of US policy towards Makarios, see Van Cofoudakis, 'American Foreign Policy and the Cyprus Problem', in Couloumbis and Iatriades, *op. cit.* in note 8, pp. 107–29.

[29] *The Guardian*, 27 October 1978.

[30] For full text of legislation, see *Greece*, No. 93, 18 August 1978 (London: Greek Press and Information Office).

[31] See commentary in *The Guardian*, 21, 22 May 1979 and *International Herald Tribune*, 12 June 1979.

[32] Information provided by Yannos Kranidiotis, 'The Negotiations for the Solution of the Cyprus Issue, 1974–81' in a collective volume on *Cyprus* (Athens: Kollaros, 1982), pp. 649–60.

[33] These questions will not be discussed at any length here because they are covered in detail in Wilson (*op. cit.* in Ch. 1, note 10).

[34] Turkey has extended her own territorial sea limit to twelve miles in the Black Sea.

[35] See joint Brussels Communiqué of 31 May 1975 to resolve problems peacefully 'by means of negotiations and as regards the continental shelf [through] the International Court'. In February 1976 Turkey rejected a Greek proposal for a non-recourse-to-force pact.

[36] *Op. cit.* in Ch. 1, note 10.

[37] See C. Rozakis, 'Two Footnotes in the Discussion on Greek Reintegration' (in Greek), *Ikonomia Kai Kinonia*, No. 15, December 1980, pp. 42–3.

[38] A mimeographed paper circulated by the Greek Ministry for Foreign Affairs in 1979.

[39] For an analysis of American influence in Greece during the Civil War period see Michael Mark Amen, 'American Institutional Penetration into Greek Military and Political Policy-making Structures: June 1947–October 1949', in *Journal of the Hellenic Diaspora*, Vol. V, No. 3, Fall 1978, pp. 89–113. 'One does not gain the impression that members of Greek authoritative society participated on an equal or significant footing with Americans in creating policies' (p. 112).

[40] Maurice Goldbloom, 'United States Policy in Post-War Greece', in R. Clogg and G. Yannopoulos, *Greece Under Military Rule* (London: Secker and Warburg, 1972), p. 231.

[41] T. Couloumbis, *Greek Political Reaction to American and NATO Influences* (New Haven: Yale University Press, 1966), pp. 33–89.

[42] *Ibid.*, p. 201.

[43] Thanos Veremis, 'Union of the Democratic Centre', in H. R. Penniman (ed.), *Greece at the Polls* (Washington DC: American Enterprise Insititute, 1981), pp. 87–8.

[44] Goldbloom, *op. cit.* in note 40, p. 236.

[45] *Ibid.*, p. 247.

[46] *Ibid.*, pp. 240–57; T. Couloumbis, J. A. Petropulos and H. Psomiades, *Foreign Interference in Greek Politics* (New York: Pella Publishing Co., 1976), pp. 129–39.

[47] This point of view was communicated to the author between 1967 and 1969 by officers who had served in the Greek contingent in Cyprus.

[48] See an appraisal by Stern, *op. cit.* in note 23, pp. 81–2.

[49] In the autumn of 1974 a middle-ranking officer who had served in Cyprus reiterated this position to the author: 'If Makarios had died, Clerides would have legally succeeded him and the Turkish invasion would have been averted'. Glafkos Clerides, the Speaker of the House and successor under the 1960 constitution to the President, was favoured by the Americans.

[50] The 'Post-mortem of the Intelligence Community of Cyprus', released on 1 October 1975, quoted in Couloumbis *et al.*, *op. cit.* in note 46, p. 140.

[51] On 13 August 1974 the State Department took a favourable position on the Turkish claims in the dispute. According to the public briefings of that day: 'We recognize that the position of the Turkish community on Cyprus requires considerable improvement and protection. We have supported a greater degree of autonomy for them.' Quoted in Stern, *op. cit.* in note 23, p. 132.

[52] The bilateral agreement of 1961 prohibited the use of American weapons against Cyprus or any other country without the consent of the President.

[53] E. Hadzipetros, 'Through a Glass Darkly', in *The Athenian*, May 1982, pp. 15–17.

[54] Concerning the negotiations, see *Kathimerini*, 16 April, 30 May, 5 and 12 June 1981; *To Vima*, 23 April, 3 May, 12 June 1981; *International Herald Tribune*, 6–7 June 1981; A. Velios, *Mesimvrini*, 1 July 1981.

[55] Marvine Howe, 'Greece Seeks to Repair Strained Ties to West', *International Herald Tribune*, 27 April 1982.

[56] *To Vima*, 28 May 1982; *Pulse*, No. 4625–22, 31 May 1982.

## Chapter III

1. A. Elephantis, 'PASOK and the Elections of 1977: The Rise of the Populist Movement', in H. R. Penniman (*op. cit.* in Chap. II, note 43), p. 112.
2. PASOK's most important views on foreign policy issues are expressed in a Party manual containing speeches of Andreas Papandreou (in Greek), *PASOK in the International Scene* (Athens, 1978), pp. 5–48.
3. See records of Parliamentary discussions – Session MH', 16 January 1979, pp. 1,675–83. Also PASOK's newspaper *Exormisi*, 4 March 1979, for the decision of the party's Central Committee concerning policy issues.
4. *To Vima*, 26 April 1981.
5. See speeches in Parliament by Karamanlis, 19 December 1977 and 19 January 1979.
6. The abolition of the Monarchy in 1974 had also deprived the Centre Union of a potent political slogan.
7. Nicos. C. Alivizatos, 'The Greek Army in the Late Forties: Towards an Institutional Autonomy', *Journal of the Hellenic Diaspora*, Vol. V, No. 3, Fall 1978, pp. 40–41.
8. *Ibid.*, pp. 42–3.
9. Thirty years after the civil war, the armed forces retain certain rights and activities which have nothing to do with the military profession, for example a radio and television station, a bank (General Bank) and a construction agency.
10. G. Karayannis, *The Drama of Greece: Glories and Miseries, IDEA, 1940–1952 (To Dramatis Ellados: Epikai Athliotites, IDEA, 1940–1952)* (Athens: published by the author), p. 206.
11. *Ibid.*
12. N. Stavrou, *Allied Policy and Military Interventions. The Political Role of the Greek Military* (Athens: Papazissis, 1976), pp. 127–8. Stavrou rightly points out the responsibility of politicians who never took seriously accusations against right-wing military associations.
13. *Ibid.*, p. 214.
14. N. Pantelakis, *L'Armée dans la Société Grecque Contemporaine*', Thèse pour le doctorat du 3ème cycle de sociologie, Université René Descartes (Paris V) 1980, pp. 74–5.
15. *To Vima*, 18 and 20 January 1976.
16. A. Spanidis, *Kathimerini*, 16 March 1975 and 18 January 1976.
17. *Ibid.*, 18 January 1976.
18. P. Loucakos, 'The Control of Political Authority over the Armed Forces', *Synchrona Themata*, October 1980, pp. 37–8.
19. *Ibid.*, pp. 38–9.
20. This is the view of Loucakos, *op.cit.* in note 18.
21. Spanidis, *op.cit.* in note 16, 18 January 1976.
22. Loucakos, *op.cit.* in note 18, p. 40.
23. L. and M. Papayannakis, 'A Comparative Study of South-European Economies' (in Greek), *Politis*, No. 9, February 1977, pp. 12–37. See also *Greece*, No. 100, 15 December 1978 (London: Greek Press and Information Office).
24. Papers of M. Papayannakis and S. Papaspiliopoulos in the Conference on 'Development or Underdevelopment: Greece' (London School of Economics, 16–17 March 1979).
25. Remittances have covered 42 per cent of the deficit. Tourism and foreign loans cover the rest.
26. T. Yannitsis, 'Problems of Greek Development' (in Greek), *Iconomia kai Kinonia*, May 1979, pp. 26–45.
27. L. Minard, 'Greece Goes Left', *Forbes Magazine*, 28 September 1981, p. 36.
28. *Financial Times*, 6 July 1982.
29. S. Papaspiliopoulos, 'Entry or not into the EEC. A False Dilemma' (in Greek) from *EEC, Greece, Mediterranean* (Athens: Nea Synora, 1978), p.93.

## Chapter IV

1. For details see *Greece*, No. 135, 2 April 1981. See also a critical article by J. K. Mazarakis-Anian, *To Vima*, 13 March 1981.
2. *Pulse*, 9 March 1981.
3. Among other Greek dailies, see *Mesimvrini*, 16 April 1981.
4. *To Vima*, 23 December 1980. See also A. Velios, 'On a Razor's Edge', in *Mesimvrini*, 27 December 1980.
5. Y. Roubatis, 'The United States and the Operational Responsibilities of the Greek Armed Forces, 1947–1987', in the *Journal of the Hellenic Diaspora*, Vol VI, No. 1, Spring 1979, pp. 46–7.
6. 'The European Community and the Greek–Turkish Dispute', *Journal of Common Market Studies*, XIX, 1980, pp. 50–51.
7. Stanley Hoffman, 'The Unhappy Choice', *New York Review of Books*, 20 November 1980.
8. David Watt, 'Europe and America', *The Economist*, 11 October 1980.
9. Interview with Gen. Bernard Rogers (SACEUR), 'Europe's Risky Drift towards Neutralism', *US News and World Report*, 15 June 1981, pp. 25–6.
10. Tass News Agency, 29 December 1975.
11. Marian K. Leighton, *Graeco–Turkish Friction: Changing Balance in the Eastern Mediterranean*, Conflict Studies No. 109 (London: Institute for the Study of Conflict, July 1979), p. 7.
12. Brown, *op.cit.* in Ch. I, note 9, p. 6.
13. *Kathimerini*, editorial of 26 September 1979.
14. *The Athenian*, April 1981, p. 41.
15. For a most precise account of Soviet–Turkish relations, see Duygu Bazoglu Sezer, *Turkey's Security Policies*, Adelphi Paper No. 164 (London: IISS, 1981), pp. 31–6.
16. *Kathimerini*, editorial of 16 April 1981.
17. Brown, *op.cit.* in Ch. I, note 9, pp. 13–14 (and relevant sources quoted).
18. J. Snyder, 'Strengthening the NATO Alliance', *Naval War College Review*, March–April 1981, pp. 33–4.
19. *Greece and Turkey: Some Military Implications Related to NATO and the Middle East* (Washington DC: Congressional Research Service, 28 February 1975), pp. 14–15.
20. Although varying in degree and kind, the demand for more autonomy in the pursuit of national policy has been the common denominator in the public statements of all major political forces in Greece. The daily *Kathimerini*, abandoning its pre-Junta editorial policy of unqualified reliance on the West, now offers through its effective editorials words of caution to the US on American policy towards Greece.
21. See A. Papandreou's interview with the *Financial*

*Times*, 24 February 1982.
22 T. Couloumbis, *The Structures of Greek Foreign Policy* (unpublished Paper presented at King's College London, January 1981), p.18.
23 The seven-to-ten ratio regulating US military aid to Greece and Turkey was questioned by American officials in the Winter of 1981/2.
24 *To Vima*, 20 April 1978.

25 A. G. Platias and R. J. Rydell, 'International Security Regimes: the Case of a Balkan Nuclear-Free Zone' in D. Carlton and C. Schaerf, *Arms Control in the 80s* (London: Macmillan, 1982), p. 289.
26 *Kathimerini*, leader article, 28 May 1981.
27 H. Macdonald, 'NATO's Dilemma: Defence, Security and Arms Control', *Millenium*, Journal of International Studies, Vol. 9, No. 2 , Autumn 1980.

# ADELPHI PAPERS

*The following is a selection of those available. They may be ordered from the Institute at a current price of* **£2.50 ($5.00)**, *post free (by Accelerated Surface Post or Bulk Air Mail to non-UK destinations).*

| | |
|---|---|
| No. 134. | THE DIFFUSION OF POWER. II: CONFLICT AND CONTROL. Papers from the IISS 18th Annual Conference. Spring 1977. |
| No. 135. | BALKAN SECURITY by F. Stephen Larrabee. Spring 1977. |
| No. 136. | OIL AND SECURITY: PROBLEMS AND PROSPECTS OF IMPORTING COUNTRIES by Edward N. Krapels. Summer 1977. |
| No. 138. | THE ROLE OF ARMS CONTROL IN THE MIDDLE EAST by Yair Evron. Autumn 1977. |
| No. 139. | SEA POWER AND WESTERN SECURITY: THE NEXT DECADE by Worth H. Bagley. Winter 1977. |
| No. 143. | A SEA OF TROUBLES? SOURCES OF DISPUTE IN THE NEW OCEAN REGIME by Barry Buzan. Spring 1978. |
| No. 147/8. | DECISION-MAKING IN SOVIET WEAPONS PROCUREMENT by Arthur J. Alexander. Winter 1978/79. *This title is a special double issue: price* **£5.00 ($10.00).** |
| No. 150. | SOVIET PERSPECTIVES ON SECURITY by Helmut Sonnenfeldt and William G. Hyland. Spring 1979. |
| No. 151. | PROSPECTS OF SOVIET POWER IN THE 1980s: PART I: Papers from the IISS 20th Annual Conference. Summer 1979. |
| No. 152. | PROSPECTS OF SOVIET POWER IN THE 1980s: PART II: Papers from the IISS 20th Annual Conference. Summer 1979. |
| No. 153. | CONGRESSIONAL POWER: IMPLICATIONS FOR AMERICAN SECURITY POLICY by Richard Haass. Summer 1979. |
| No. 154. | GLOBALISM OR REGIONALISM? UNITED STATES POLICY TOWARDS SOUTHERN AFRICA by Garrick Utley. Winter 1979/80. |
| No. 155. | THE AEGEAN DISPUTE by Andrew Wilson. Winter 1979/80. |
| No. 156. | THE FUTURE OF BRITAIN'S DETERRENT FORCE by Peter Nailor and Jonathan Alford. Spring 1980. |
| No. 157. | SOVIET POLICY TOWARDS IRAN AND THE GULF by Shahram Chubin. Spring 1980. |
| No. 158. | SAUDI ARABIA'S SEARCH FOR SECURITY by Adeed Dawisha. Spring 1980. |
| No. 159. | SOUTH AFRICA'S NARROWING SECURITY OPTIONS by Robert S. Jaster. Spring 1980. |
| No. 160. | THE FUTURE OF STRATEGIC DETERRENCE: PART I: Papers from the IISS 21st Annual Conference. Winter 1980. |
| No. 161. | THE FUTURE OF STRATEGIC DETERRENCE: PART II: Papers from the IISS 21st Annual Conference. Winter 1980. |
| No. 162. | CONFLICT AND REGIONAL ORDER IN SOUTH-EAST ASIA by Michael Leifer. Winter 1980. |
| No. 163. | A PALESTINIAN STATE: EXAMINING THE ALTERNATIVES by Avi Plascov. Spring 1981. |
| No. 164. | TURKEY'S SECURITY POLICIES by Duygu Bazoglu Sezer. Spring 1981. |
| No. 165. | THE FUTURE OF ARMS CONTROL: PART IV: THE IMPACT OF WEAPONS TEST RESTRICTIONS by Farooq Hussain. Spring 1981. |
| No. 166. | THIRD-WORLD CONFLICT AND INTERNATIONAL SECURITY: PART I: Papers from the IISS 22nd Annual Conference. Summer 1981. |
| No. 167. | THIRD-WORLD CONFLICT AND INTERNATIONAL SECURITY: PART II: Papers from the IISS 22nd Annual Conference. Summer 1981. |
| No. 168. | NUCLEAR WEAPONS IN EUROPE by Gregory Treverton. Summer 1981. |
| No. 169. | CAN NUCLEAR WAR BE CONTROLLED? by Desmond Ball. Autumn 1981. |
| No. 170. | GERMANY AND THE WESTERN ALLIANCE: LESSONS FROM THE 1980 CRISES by Philip Windsor. Autumn 1981. |
| No. 171. | THE SPREAD OF NUCLEAR WEAPONS: MORE MAY BE BETTER by Kenneth N. Waltz. Autumn 1981. |
| No. 172. | CHINA AND SOUTH-EAST ASIA: STRATEGIC INTERESTS AND POLICY PROSPECTS by Takashi Tajima. Winter 1981. |
| No. 173. | AMERICA'S SECURITY IN THE 1980s: PART I: Papers from the IISS 23rd Annual Conference, Spring 1982. |
| No. 174. | AMERICA'S SECURITY IN THE 1980s: PART II: Papers from the IISS 23rd Annual Conference, Spring 1982. |
| No. 175. | DETERRENCE IN THE 1980s PART I: AMERICAN STRATEGIC FORCES AND EXTENDED DETERRENCE by Anthony H. Cordesman. Summer 1982. |
| No. 176. | MBFR: LESSONS AND PROBLEMS by Lothar Ruehl. Summer 1982. |
| No. 177. | ARMS CONTROL AND THE POLITICS OF EUROPEAN SECURITY by Theodor H. Winkler. Autumn 1982. |
| No. 178. | THE EVOLUTION OF JAPANESE SECURITY POLICY by Yukio Satoh. Autumn 1982. |

*Discount rates are available for bulk orders of 11 or more Papers of the same title.*